A SHOW OF HANDS

A SHOW OF *H*ANDS

NEEDLEPOINT DESIGNS
BY JANET McCAFFERY

WITH NANCY LINDEMEYER

PHOTOGRAPHS BY STARR OCKENGA
DESIGNED BY KATHLEEN HERLIHY-PAOLI
TEXT BY CIBA VAUGHAN

HEARST BOOKS
NEW YORK

The painting appearing on page 12, *Mother with Three Daughters,* ca. 1845, is reproduced by permission of the Chrysler Museum, Norfolk, Virginia. Gift of Edgar William and Bernice Chrysler Garbisch, 76.53.2b.

The following paintings are reproduced by permission of The Abby Aldrich Rockefeller Folk Art Center, Williamsburg, Virginia:
Page 17: Portrait of Deborah Glen, artist anonymous, 1700s.
Page 34: *Boy with Finch,* by John Brewster, Jr., ca. 1880.
Page 55: *Girl Holding Cherries,* by Robert Lottridge Dorr, ca. 1814.
Page 90: *The Merchant,* by R. B. Crafft, 1836.

It is the policy of William Morrow and Company, Inc., and its imprints and affiliates, recognizing the importance of preserving what has been written, to print the books we publish on acid-free paper, and we exert our best efforts to that end.

Library of Congress Cataloging–in–Publication Data

McCaffery, Janet.
A show of hands: needlepoint designs/ by Janet McCaffery, with Nancy Lindemeyer; photographs by Starr Ockenga.
p. cm.
ISBN 0-688-11297-8
1. Canvas embroidery—Patterns. I. Lindemeyer, Nancy.
II.Title.
TT778.C3M37 1994 94-13327
746.44'2041—dc20 CIP

Printed in the United States of America

First Edition

1 2 3 4 5 6 7 8 9 10

BOOK DESIGN BY KATHLEEN HERLIHY-PAOLI, INKSTONE DESIGN

This book is dedicated to my Dear Dan

ACKNOWLEDGMENTS

I would like to express my heartfelt thanks to the following people, whose talent, knowledge, interest, and enthusiasm helped put this book together.

First, thanks to my dear and patient friend Inger Fisher, who first taught me how to needlepoint. I'll forever cherish the many hours we spent stitching and laughing together. My special thanks to Nancy Lindemeyer, editor of *Victoria Magazine*, needlework aficionado and longtime friend, whose vision, encouragement, goodwill, and practical support made this book possible.

I am also particularly grateful to Ann Bramson, my editor at William Morrow, who offered the rare gift of allowing me the freedom to be myself in this undertaking, and thanks, too, to all Ann's associates at William Morrow, who helped to turn this project into a book.

I am especially indebted to photographer Starr Ockenga for her exceptional dedica-tion and professionalism and her endless generosity in sharing both her treasures and her expertise. Her gorgeous photographs for this book are everything that I hoped for and more than I could have imagined.

Thanks, too, to Starr's associate, lighting expert Stefan Hagen, for his technical expertise and his saintly patience.

For transforming my stitcheries into book form, I want to thank Ciba Vaughan for her nurturing support, intelligent organizational skills, and happy ability to turn my ramblings and reminiscences into a coherent text to accompany the designs. Thanks, too, to book designer Kathleen Herlihy-Paoli for her keen sense of design, attention to detail, and unflagging spirit of cooperation. Judie Phipps, the most positive and dependable of colleagues and a consummate professional when it comes to needlepoint, was responsible (along with her wonderful coterie of expert stitchers in Iowa) for completing borders, backgrounds, and finishing for many of the designs in this book. Dear and loyal friend Jane Resnick stitched up the butterfly design while on vacation, and multitalented New York bookbinder Barbara Mauriello labored long and lovingly to mount several of my stitchery designs on boxes, book fronts, and albums. I could never have completed all the projects for *A Show of Hands* in time to meet the publisher's deadline without their help.

Many people contributed to the style and whimsy of the photographic settings for these needlepoint designs; chief among them is Susan George Calsmer, to whom I am indebted for her wonderful selection of props and unbounded enthusiasm for the book project. My dear neighbor Eli Fendelman generously lent assorted treasures to accompany the photograph of the child's scrapbook on page 75. Special thanks go to the "Ladies on the Lawn" of the Chilmark Methodist Church in Martha's Vineyard, at whose weekly summer flea market I acquired many of my dearest treasures and much of the design inspiration for this book. Chief among them are Jane N. Slater, Sue Miller, Barbara Dunn, Greta Ghee, and Sue Parks—all of whom cheerfully shared their knowledge and enthusiasm for old and quirky items with me over the years.

Thanks, too, to shop owners Susan Parrish, Elaine Friedman, and Donald Hillman —all of New York City—for lending many of their special antique treasures for photography. All three shops are inspirational, and each has provided some of my favorite oddments over the years.

Finally, my loving thanks to Daniel Schwartz for his daily patience and unstinting support, which enabled me to spend the time and energy necessary to bring this book to fruition—and to my mother, Florence Metzger, and my brother and sister-in-law, Lou and Pat Metzger, for their constant love and encouragement as I sketched and stitched my way through *A Show of Hands*.

CONTENTS

PREFACE

by Nancy Lindemeyer

𝓘T SEEMS THAT JANET McCAFFERY AND I HAVE TALKED FOR years about her doing a needlepoint book—and here it is. But, of course, as I should have known when those discourses over tea cups took place in her marvelous studio, the book has not turned out exactly as I expected. Janet's work follows her own determined views. And thank goodness, or we would not have this unique assemblage.

𝒪NE OF MY PLEASURES OVER THE YEARS OF OUR FRIENDSHIP HAS been to visit Janet, either in her studio stacked to the rafters with art books, antique fabrics, and wallpapers or in her home, where glass jars most of us would store cookies in are filled instead with glistening ornaments. My eye has always wandered to the objects of her desire as we have talked and worked. Her enthusiasm for an old sugar and creamer set bought at a church lawn sale on Martha's Vineyard always held me in awe. Her mother taught her to pick up a piece of china or crockery and appraise its value. But that value is hardly monetary for Janet. What is important to her is what pleases her, what her mind can add to her ever-growing design lexicon.

𝓕OR NEEDLEPOINTERS, JANET'S WORK IS PURE inspiration. A bravura blend of color and texture, the designs in this book are instructional as well. She is coaxing us along, her hand on ours. Her "show of hands" is a striking example of how compositions take shape, from the simple to the exquisitely complex. One may take an element of a design and use it as

THE LITTLE BOX DECOUPAGED WITH BITS OF VICTORIAN SCRAP, ABOVE, AND ANTIQUE BOTANICAL PRINTS, BELOW, ARE AMONG JANET'S DESIGN SOURCES.

the basis of one's own creativity. Joy and enthusiasm abound in the designs. Perhaps that is the most important trademark of all for Janet McCaffery. But before I become too comfortable with the idea of joy and enthusiasm, I must add perfection. Borders must meet her meticulous standards, even if it means hours of restitching and designing. And colors have often meant yarn studies, which have gone on for days. So readers and needlepointers will have an even greater insider's view, I can tell you that she steered her own course very carefully, knowing when not to stop. By that I mean that designing and creativity continued until her hand studies were complete for her mind's eye. Would one toy have been enough in the designs on pages 73-75? Perhaps, but not for Janet. As we can see in the finished result, not for us either.

COLOR STUDIES, SCRAPS OF STITCHED BORDER PATTERNS, AND SWATCHES OF INSPIRATIONAL FABRIC FILL JANET'S STUDIO.

*J*ANET AND I BECAME ASSOCIATES SOME YEARS AGO BECAUSE we both found ourselves in love with the best of the past. Some designers have chosen to replicate motifs and designs, while Janet has followed a different route, taking from her studies in art museums and fabric collections what is compelling. She then creates, reinterpreting in her stitchery an essence and an individual vision. Her background as an illustrator is definitely seen in this process of recomposition, giving us the touchstone but then leading us somewhere different, somewhere we have not been before.

*S*O I WILL END AS I HAVE BEGUN, WITH THE UNEXPECTED nature of this book and the unique vision of its subject. Readers will come very close to having the experience I have had with Janet—of sitting over tea drunk from her mother's cups and being intimately involved in what she is about, what she so generously shares, and what she has so meticulously crafted for all our pleasure. I can think of nothing more pleasant for those of us who love the past, love to stitch, and delight in design.

INTRODUCTION

*A*S A WORKING ARTIST, I'VE HAPPILY DESIGNED HUNDREDS OF PROJECTS OVER THE YEARS—BUT ALWAYS TO FILL AN ORDER TO PLEASE A CLIENT. PUTTING TOGETHER *A SHOW OF HANDS* HAS BEEN AN EXHILARATING NEW ADVENTURE FOR ME. CREATING A COLLECTION OF NEEDLEPOINT DESIGNS JUST TO PLEASE MYSELF, I FOLLOWED MY WHIMSY TO FILL THESE PAGES. COME SEE WHERE IT LEADS!

NINETEENTH-CENTURY PICTURE BOOKS AND FOLK ART PAINTINGS ARE AMONG THE MYRIAD SOURCES I MINED TO CREATE THE HANDS THAT APPEAR IN THE DESIGNS IN THIS BOOK.

LIKE MOST ARTISTS, I ALWAYS TRAVEL WITH SKETCHBOOK IN hand, ever on the alert for inspiration. Several years ago, when I wandered into a wonderful exhibition called "A Celebration of Childhood" at the Museum of American Folk Art in New York, inspiration struck with a vengeance. I was enthralled by the naive portraits of children and families that filled the gallery. Though most were painted in the nineteenth century, at the height of the Victorian era, these portraits were neither frilly nor frivolous. They were simple, personal, direct, and filled with quirky details and vibrant colors that thrilled my soul. I was especially intrigued by the fact that each figure, young or old, clasped something symbolic in hand.

EAGERLY, I SKETCHED PAGE AFTER PAGE OF MOTIFS AND patterns as I moved from portrait to portrait. Only when I finally quit the show did I realize that I'd drawn nothing but hands, each winsomely cuffed and each holding an object that had caught my fancy, from sprigs of

flowers and sprays of fruit to family pets and childhood treasures. I knew I would someday do something with this treasure trove of drawings, but it was nearly a decade before I turned to them again.

WHEN I WAS INVITED TO CREATE a book of original needlepoint designs, the hand sketches leaped to mind. Soon I was researching other American folk art portraits of the period, scouting out appropriate gestures, decorative cuffs, and appealing items for my needlepoint hands to hold. At home and in my studio, I'm surrounded by things I love, things that buoy my spirit from day to day. Shelves and walls are crammed with gaily printed scraps of fabric, woven ribbons and hand-blocked wallpaper, antique china, funny postcards, old book illustrations and kids' artless doodles, plus odds and ends of texture and pattern that have charmed me over the years. One way or another, many of these favorite things found their way into my stitcheries.

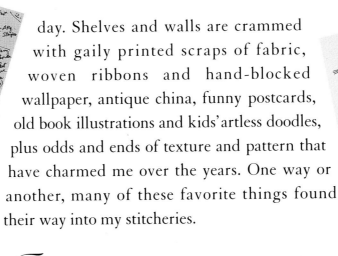

Though the pieces in this book were inspired by aspects of American folk art portraits, *inspiration*—as in "a point of departure"—is the operative word. I've made no attempt to reproduce any element of a particular painting exactly, nor was I concerned with historical—or even anatomical—accuracy. The hands are decorative elements, as are the objects they hold. I've rarely used more than two stitches—outline and basketweave—to create my designs. My finished "sewings" will never win awards for technical excellence, yet mastering even the minimum skills of needlepoint has opened up whole new creative worlds to me. After twenty years of simple stitching, I've yet to exhaust my enthusiasm for plying the needle! By sharing that creative process along with my designs in this book, I hope to share that pleasure with you as well.

A few technical notes: In creating this collection of "hand portraits," I arbitrarily chose to make most of the fifteen major designs in the same approximate size (14 x 14 inches square), to stitch each on the same gauge canvas (number 12 mono), and to limit my palette to approximately twenty colors for most designs. Charts and instructions for major designs appear at the end of each chapter, but throughout the book, you'll find suggestions and samples of alternative ways to interpret each pattern. I hope and expect you'll come up with variations of your own.

MATCHING YARN SAMPLES (LEFT) TO PENCILED SKETCHES (ABOVE) IS AMONG THE MOST EXACTING STEPS IN NEEDLEPOINT DESIGN. INSPIRATION FROM WELL-LOVED BITS AND PIECES I'VE COLLECTED OVER THE YEARS, LIKE THE ANTIQUE CREAMER BELOW, SPARKED THE FINAL CHOICE OF COLORS AND PATTERNS FOR EVERY DESIGN IN THIS COLLECTION.

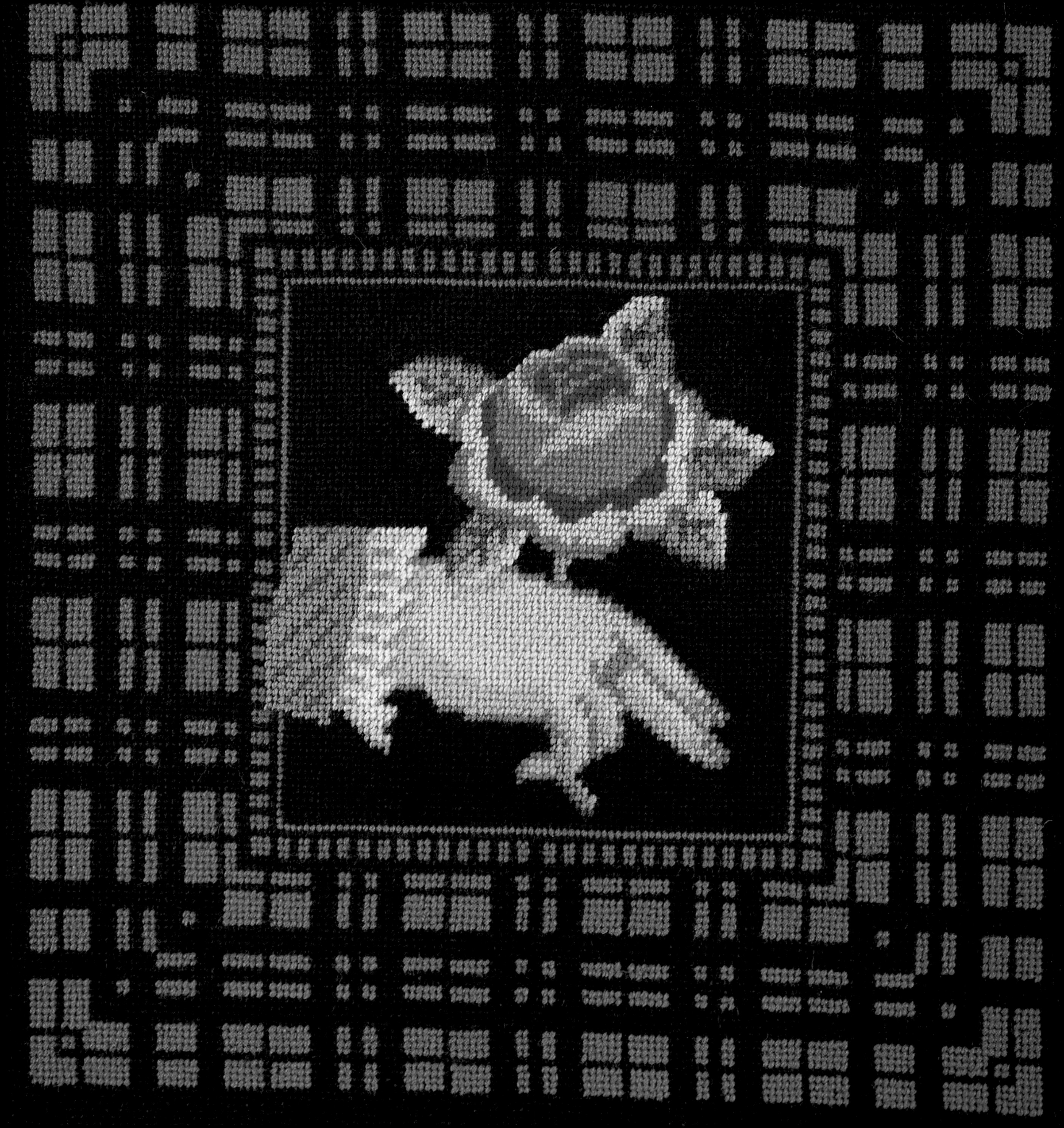

Chapter One

BIRTH OF A DESIGN

G ERTRUDE STEIN ONCE SAID THAT "A ROSE IS A ROSE IS A ROSE," BUT I BEG TO DIFFER! PAINTED OR STITCHED, EACH ARTIST'S ROSE IS AS UNIQUE AS A LIVING BLOSSOM. SINCE IT IS BOTH MY FAVORITE FLOWER AND A RECURRING MOTIF IN THE FOLK ART PORTRAITS THAT INSPIRED THIS BOOK, I OFFER YOU MY OWN NEEDLE- POINT ROSE TO OPEN THIS COLLECTION.

EXQUISITE CHENILLE STITCHERY ON MY ANTIQUE JEWELRY BOX (RIGHT) AND SHADINGS ON A FRAGILE SILK ROSE FROM A NEIGHBORHOOD SHOP (ABOVE) HELPED ME SHAPE THE PETALS FOR MY NEEDLEPOINT BLOSSOM. THE JAUNTY PAIR OF KNITTED STOCKINGS, BELOW, HANG ON THE WALL IN MY STUDIO. TAKING A FRESH GLANCE AT THESE OLD FRIENDS ONE DAY, I STUMBLED ONTO THE COLOR SCHEME FOR THIS DESIGN!

𝓘'VE ALWAYS LOVED ROSES— not the too-perfect, long-stemmed, store-bought kind, but the lush, old-fashioned roses that bloom in the gardens of my dreams. In fact, when I began to work on this book, I was startled to discover just how many of my personal treasures celebrate this beautiful flower. Rose-patterned pottery and stacks of rose-figured fabrics line my shelves, rose motif paintings fill my walls, and rose-bedecked knickknacks spill from every nook and cranny in my studio! Inspiration enough for a whole bouquet of designs— the challenge was to craft a single rose that would honor them all.

𝒯O MY DELIGHT, I FOUND THAT MANY NINETEENTH-CENTURY artists shared my passion for roses. Proper Victorians seemed to prize this flower above all others. Roses of every hue and description were planted in their gardens, celebrated in their paintings, appliquéd on quilts, embroidered on doilies, and needlepointed in rich profusion onto carpets, footstools, and dainty cushions. According to custom, the rose betokened beauty, innocence, love, and commitment. What better symbol, then, to grace a young woman's portrait, be she bride, wife, sister, or mother? Or so many artists must have believed, for the number of early portraits of girls and women with rose in hand is truly astonishing. (A charming example is pictured at right).

𝓗AVING PICKED THE ROSE AS THE FIRST "PORTRAIT" MOTIF OF the collection, I made dozens of colored pencil sketches to work out the precise gesture of the hand (should it be offering the rose or holding it fast?) and the size and shape and shade of the flower itself (a single blossom or a small bouquet?). What patterns to pick for the background and borders (plain or figured? striped or plaid?). My first pen-cilings were rendered in pastel shades (too bland). I moved on to rich, jewel-toned hues (too serious), and finally settled on a brilliant American Beauty pink and rich Cobalt Blue palette that struck just the exuber-ant note I was after.

𝒩EXT, THE TRIAL AND ERROR PHASE OF STITCHING BEGAN: ONE can only do so many sketches, then it's time to dig into the yarn. To be truthful, I never really do a finished sketch; I need to save a bit of my creative energy for the stitching. Certain problems have to be worked out right on the canvas—otherwise there's no magic, no spontaneity to the design.

ℬEFORE TAKING NEEDLE IN HAND, I FIRST SKETCH THE outline of my provisional design onto the canvas in waterproof pen, then plunge directly into the stitching. Wool stitches on canvas have a texture and luminosity that is quite different from penciled colors on paper, so at this stage I always keep skeins of yarn in various shades of each color I plan to use close by as I work the design, stitching in first lighter and then darker bits of yarn and patiently plucking them out again until I find a combination of colors that makes me happy.

ℋERE, FOR THE FIRST BUT NOT THE LAST TIME IN THESE pages, I want to remind you that color is a very personal thing—there are no right and wrong colors, only colors that please an indi-vidual eye. Each design in this book is stitched in colors that make *me* deliriously happy, but feel free to substitute colors that make your own heart sing.

ONE OF THE JOYS OF CREATING YOUR OWN needlepoint designs is the freedom it gives to shift, shuffle, alter, or recombine elements of the design to suit your fancy. Here and on the following pages—using my rose portrait as a workshop example—I suggest a few reworkings of my original design in the hope that you'll be inspired to fiddle on your own. Options explored and initially rejected in my first tentative sketches (left), resurfaced in some of the designs developed during this second go-round. No sketch should ever be discarded!

IN MY ORIGINAL PEN-
CIL SKETCHES (ABOVE),
I WORKED HARD TO
REDUCE EACH ELE-
MENT OF THE DESIGN
DOWN TO AN ELEGANT
SIMPLICITY.

I FIRST HAD MY NEEDLEPOINTED ROSE-IN-hand portrait finished as a cushion. (See Chapter Six for tips on finishing.) Once I saw how beautiful the finished pillow looked, I set to work stitching the identical plaid border around a square of solid blue to make a companion pillow. Though I opted to leave the center of this second piece blank (right), I could just as easily have filled the square with a monogram (see page 24) or stitched in a favorite motto (using the charted alphabets that appear in Chapter Six). Next time, perhaps.

TURNING TO THE ROSE ITSELF, I PLOTTED IN AN EXTRA LEAF or two, extended the stem, and let the flower take center stage on the diminutive cushion at left, framed only by the simple inset border copied from the original design. For the commemorative wreath (framed on page 15 and stitched into a pillow, lower right), I turned the original rose on its side, overlapped five of my basic leaf shapes into a gentle arc, and stitched the circular pattern in petit point (on number 18 gauge canvas) for extra definition, adding a smattering of navy blue dots to give the background a hint of texture.

$\mathcal{I}$F IT'S TRUE, AS THE NINETEENTH-CENTURY POET JOHN BOYLE O'Reilly said, that

The red rose whispers of passion,
And the white rose breathes of love

then this luscious pink rose embodies the spirit of both—the perfect mix for a wedding day.

$\mathcal{I}$N FASHIONING MY ROSE WREATH DESIGN INTO A COVER INSET for the wedding album pictured here, I bowed to tradition and switched the background color from racy blue to a demure cream. Inside the circlet of flowers, I stitched the initials and anniversary year of the happy couple, then had the finished design framed in raw silk and handsomely mounted by Barbara Mauriello, an imaginative and accomplished bookbinder of my acquaintance. The result, I think, is a worthy gift for any occasion.

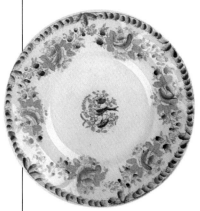

$\mathcal{H}$ERE I NEED TO ADD A WORD ABOUT FINISHING NEEDLEPOINT projects. As an artist, I loved the design phase of these sewings—sketching

shapes, selecting colors, and laboring over details until the finished stitchery was as close as possible to what I saw in my mind's eye. But once the designs were done, I welcomed the help of friends, who stitched in acres of background and yards of border patterns on assorted projects. And when each needlepointed piece design was done, I gratefuly relied on talented experts to provide each stitchery with a proper setting. It may be unfashionable in an age when many of us feel we ought to be able to do everything, but I believe in concentrating on the things I do best, and inviting others to work their own special magic thereafter.

CIRCLETS OF FLOW-
ERS—OFTEN HAND-
PAINTED BY CHILDREN
IN ENGLISH FACTO-
RIES FOR MERE PEN-
NIES A PLATE—WERE
A FAVORITE EMBEL-
LISHMENT FOR CHINA
KNICKKNACKS IN
NINETEENTH-CENTURY
AMERICAN HOMES.
THE TWO SAMPLES
ABOVE ARE TREASURES
FROM MY OWN CUP-
BOARD.
AT LEFT, A DETAIL OF THE
ROSE WREATH STITCH-
ERY IN PROGRESS.

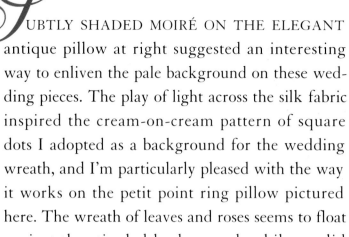

*S*UBTLY SHADED MOIRÉ ON THE ELEGANT antique pillow at right suggested an interesting way to enliven the pale background on these wedding pieces. The play of light across the silk fabric inspired the cream-on-cream pattern of square dots I adopted as a background for the wedding wreath, and I'm particularly pleased with the way it works on the petit point ring pillow pictured here. The wreath of leaves and roses seems to float against the stippled background, while a solid background of cream stitches inside the wreath lend added weight to the initials.

*A*S FOR THE TRIM OF GOLDEN CORD: GILDING THE LILY (OR THE rose, or anything else, for that matter) is not my usual style, but every needlepoint pillow, however small, deserves an appropriate edging. In this case, the gold cord finish for the little ring pillow was inspired by the gilt trim on an antique, rose-patterned porcelain taper holder in my collection (left), but I also think it's a nice complement to the golden wedding rings the pillow will bear. A touch of gold seduces the eye and seems to proclaim: "This piece is special, part of a celebration; treasure it always."

*P*ERHAPS YOU'LL THINK OF OTHER WAYS TO USE THESE ROSE designs for wedding accessories or other occasions. Petit point pillows of the single rose would make charming gifts for the bridesmaids, don't you think? And one day I'm going to stitch six squares of the rose wreath pattern together for a bedside rug.

*R*EVIEWING THE PROJECTS IN THIS FIRST CHAPTER, I HOPE YOU'LL note the ways I've used elements from one design to create new patterns, and altered the background or border colors to give each design a different look. Similar possibilities exist for all designs in this book.

$\mathscr{P}$LAIDS ARE DELICIOUS PATTERNS TO PLAY WITH, AND I COLLECT plaid swatches with the same zeal with which I gather rose motifs. Antique silk, satin, and grosgrain plaid ribbons—some with as many as a dozen different colors woven into intricate patterns no more than an inch wide—are among my special treasures. Their brilliant hues and infinitely varied designs are a continual delight and inspiration for my needlepoint.

$\mathscr{Y}$OU'LL DISCOVER THAT I'VE USED THE SAME, TWO-TONE plaid in very different colorways as the border design for several of the designs in this book, including the rose. To give you an idea of just how different that pattern can look, I translated the original blue-on-blue design into a vibrant blue and red border for the monogram pillow below.

$\mathscr{T}$HOUGH MATHEMATICS ARE NOT MY STRONG POINT, I FIND THAT plaids are easier to work out with the help of graph paper. The difficulty lies in scaling the pattern to suit a particular design. For comparison purposes, you can either plot the design in several different sizes and widths on separate sheets of graph paper, or have a single graphed plaid reproduced in a variety of sizes on the copy machine at your local copy shop. Graphed paper patterns also help in the tricky job of figuring out how to miter the corners of a plaid border. Just fold one end of the graphed border strip under at a 45-degree angle. Make several copies and fit the mitered edges together to get an idea of how the finished corners should look.

$\mathscr{T}$WO FINAL TIPS ON STITCHING THIS particular plaid: I find it easiest to work from the center of the border pattern out toward each corner, and I always stitch in the darker grid of the plaid before filling in lighter blocks.

GAILY PATTERNED PLAID RIBBONS LIKE THESE ANTIQUE SNIPPETS (ABOVE AND BELOW) ARE LIKE MINIATURE COLOR STUDIES WOVEN IN SILK. THEY'VE NOT ONLY INSPIRED THE BORDER PATTERNS FOR SOME OF MY DESIGNS, BUT THE ENTIRE COLOR PALETTE FOR OTHERS.

J.H.T.

THE PATTERNS

◆ 18 x 18-INCH SQUARE
OF NO. 12 MONO CANVAS.
◆ NO. 20 TAPESTRY NEEDLE.
◆ 3-STRAND PATERNAYAN
PERSIAN WOOL OR
OTHER NEEDLEPOINT
YARN IN THE FOLLOWING
COLORS AND APPROXI-
MATE AMOUNTS:

No.	Color	Yds.
202	Med. Gray	4
490	Med. Flesh	4
493	Pale Flesh	5
500	Dk. Federal Blue	150
502	Med. Federal Blue	2
521	Dk. Teal	4
522	Med. Teal	4
523	Lt. Teal	4
525	Lightest Teal	4
543	Med. Cobalt Blue	120
741	Tobacco	1
742	Med. Tobacco	4
744	Lt. Tobacco	4
745	Lightest Tobacco	4
863	Copper	4
903	Dk. American Beauty	3
905	Med. American Beauty	6
907	Lt. American Beauty	4
915	Dusty Pink	3

FRIENDSHIP ROSE

*T*O CREATE THE 14 x 14-INCH DESIGN PICTURED ON PAGE 14, prepare an 18 x 18-inch piece of number 12 mono canvas following instructions in Chapter Six. Bind the edges of the canvas with masking tape, and sketch in the design with permanent needlepoint markers to match yarn colors. Use two strands of yarn to stitch the design.

*R*EFERRING TO THE CHARTED PATTERN AND ACCOMPANYING color code, first outline the hand, cuff, and flower in continental stitch. Next, stitch in the ring, veins on the leaves, and stripes in the cuff; then complete the center motif in basketweave. Next, stitch the inner border in blue (note the way the cuff breaks every so slightly into the inner rim of the pattern). Stitch the plaid border, working from the center of the design out toward the corners, then complete the borders and background square. (Tips on finishing begin on page 107.)

202	490	493	500	502	521	522
523	525	543	741	742	744	745
863	903	905	907	915		

HAND W/ ROSE (COVER)

Plaid Border

—500
—543
—903
—905
—907
—915
—525
—523
—522
—521
—741
—202
—502
—742
—744
—745
—863
—490
—493

Rose

Leaves

Ring

Cuff

Lace

Flesh

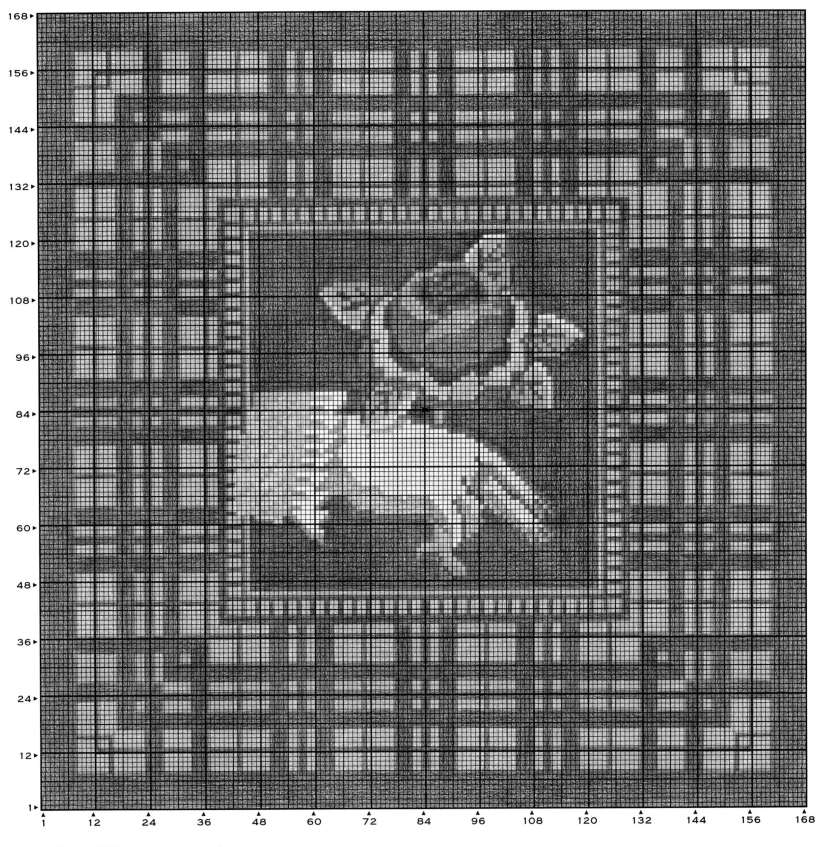

168►
156►
144►
132►
120►
108►
96►
84►
72►
60►
48►
36►
24►
12►
1►

1 12 24 36 48 60 72 84 96 108 120 132 144 156 168

✕ MIDDLE POINT

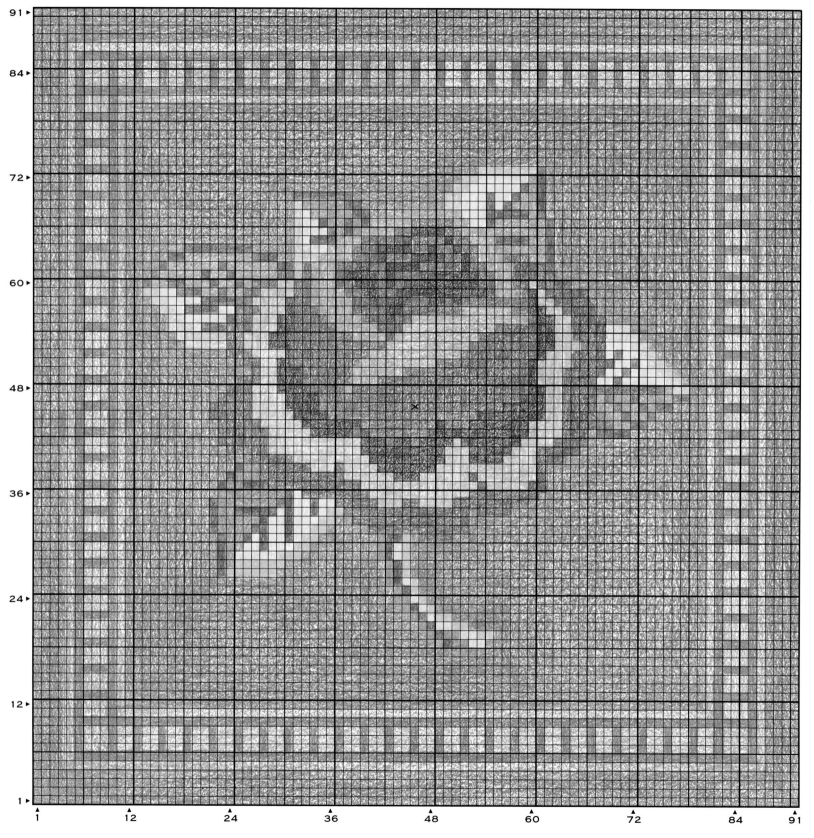

✕ MIDDLE POINT

ROSE ALONE

𝒯O COMPLETE THE 8 × 8-INCH DESIGN PICTURED ON PAGE 18, PREPARE
a 12 × 12-inch square of number 12 mono canvas following instructions in
the chapter on Basics. Bind the edges of the canvas with masking tape and
sketch in outlines of the design with permanent needlepoint markers to
match yarn colors. Use two strands of yarn to stitch the design.

𝑅EFERRING TO THE CHARTED PATTERN AND ACCOMPANYING
color code, first outline the leaves and stem in continental stitch. Outline
the rose petals in continental stitch. Complete the central motif and background in basketweave stitch.

𝒫LOT AND STITCH THE BORDER DESIGN. TO COMPLETE THE PILLOW,
consult Chapter Six. Fill the pillow with polyester fiberfill or potpourri.

500	521	522	523	525
543	903	905	907	915

WHAT YOU'LL NEED

◆ 12 x 12-INCH SQUARE
OF NO. 12 MONO CANVAS.

◆ NO. 20 TAPESTRY NEEDLE.

◆ 3-STRAND PATERNAYAN
PERSIAN WOOL OR
OTHER NEEDLEPOINT
YARN IN THE FOLLOWING
COLORS AND APPROXI-
MATE AMOUNTS:

No.	Color	Yds.
500	Dk. Federal Blue	25
521	Dk. Teal	4
522	Med. Teal	7
523	Lt. Teal	7
525	Lightest Teal	6
543	Med. Cobalt Blue	15
903	Dk. American Beauty	4
905	Med. American Beauty	7
907	Lt. American Beauty	4
915	Dusty Pink	3

◆10 x 10-INCH SQUARE
OF NO. 18 MONO CANVAS.
◆NO. 22 TAPESTRY
NEEDLE.
◆3-STRAND PATERNAYAN
PERSIAN WOOL OR OTHER
NEEDLEPOINT YARN IN
THE FOLLOWING COLORS AND
APPROXIMATE AMOUNTS:

No.	Color	Yds.
For Wreath:		
521	Dk. Teal	8
522	Med. Teal	18
523	Lt. Teal	16
525	Lightest Teal	12
903	Dk. American Beauty	5
905	Med. American Beauty	10
907	Lt. American Beauty	6
For Blue Background:		
501	Federal Blue	30
570	Navy	10
752	Old Gold	10

ROSE WREATH

*T*O CREATE THE 7 3/4 X 7 3/4-INCH PETIT POINT ROSE WREATH picture on page 15, or the petit point Rose Wreath album cover inset (page 20) or ring pillow (page 23), prepare a 10 x 10-inch piece of number 18 mono canvas following instructions in Chapter Six. Bind the edges of the canvas with masking tape and sketch in the design with permanent needlepoint markers to match yarn colors. Use a single strand of yarn to stitch the design.

*R*EFERRING TO THE CHARTED PATTERN AND ACCOMPANYING color code, first outline the roses and leaves in continental stitch; complete the motif in basketweave.

*P*LOT THE INITIALS AND/OR DATE ON GRAPH PAPER; THEN sketch and stitch them in the center of the wreath. For a blue background, stitch initials and date in Old Gold; for a creamy background, stitch initials and date in Federal Blue. Fill in the background and borders in blues or creamy light golds, using basketweave stitch. To complete a framed picture, wedding album cover, or ring pillow, refer to Chapter Six.

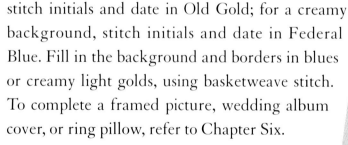

521 522 523 525 903

905 907 501 570 752

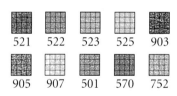

140 ▶
132 ▶
120 ▶
108 ▶
96 ▶
84 ▶
72 ▶
60 ▶
48 ▶
36 ▶
24 ▶
12 ▶
1 ▶

1   12   24   36   48   60   72   84   96   108   120   132   141

✕ MIDDLE POINT

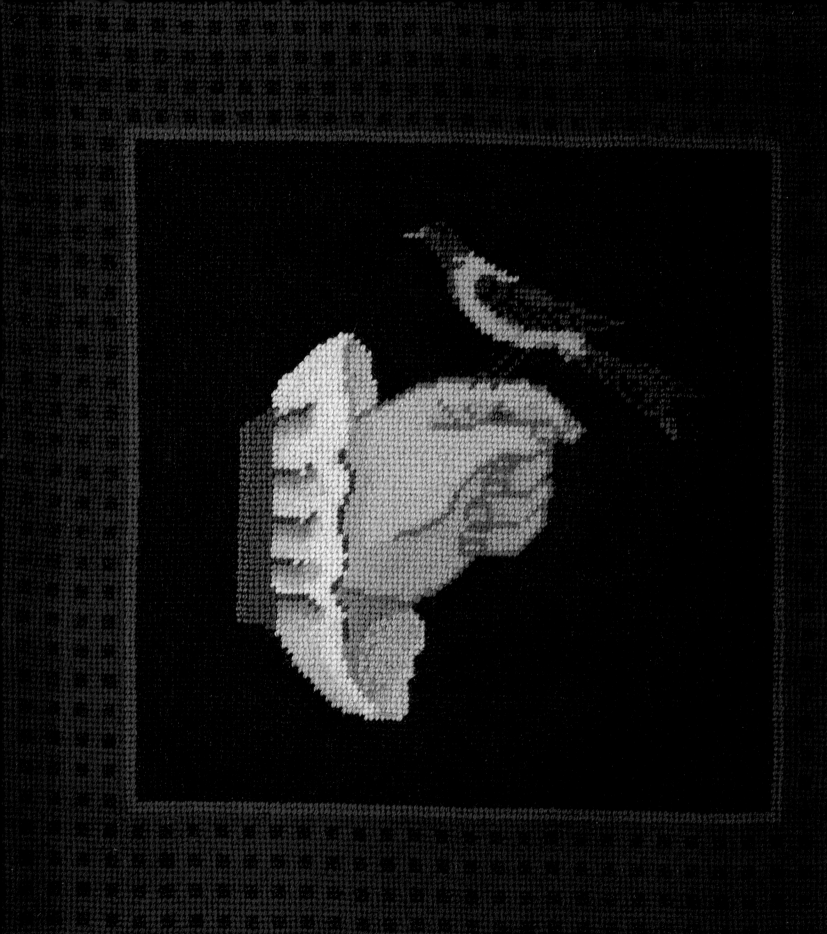

Chapter Two

THE CHALLENGE
OF COLOR

WHAT DELIGHTS MY EYE AND CHEERS MY SPIRIT IN FOLK ART IS THE UNINHIBITED AND UTTERLY PERSONAL USE OF COLOR. OFTEN SELF-TAUGHT, THESE EARLY ARTISTS USED THE SKILLS AND MATERIALS AT HAND, ATTACKED THE CANVAS WITH CONFIDENCE, AND TRUSTED THEIR INSTINCTS EVERY STEP OF THE WAY. I'VE TRIED TO DO THE SAME IN MY DESIGNS.

INSPIRED BY THE
BREWSTER PORTRAIT,
BELOW, I SNATCHED A
RUFFLE FROM THE LIT-
TLE BOY'S COLLAR TO
FRAME THE CUFF IN
MY DESIGN. DON'T BE
AFRAID TO MIX ELE-
MENTS FROM YOUR
SOURCE MATERIALS TO
SUIT YOUR OWN ARTIS-
TIC VISION.

$\mathcal{C}$OLOR IS SURELY THE MOST PERSONAL ASPECT OF NEEDLEPOINT design and the one that many of us find most daunting. With a sharp pencil and a bit of practice, anyone can trace out a pattern suitable for stitching. But the trick of choosing just the right colors for each element of the design can stymie even the most accomplished needle artist.

$\mathcal{H}$APPILY, THERE'S A LIBERATING LESSON TO BE LEARNED FROM folk art, not only from the portraits that sparked these stitcheries, but from handcrafted pieces as well. The lesson is this: There are no rules to follow, no rights and wrongs. Stitch it as *you* see it. Aim for liveliness and excitement. Choose colors to create contrast, to emphasize shape and pattern, and, above all, to please yourself. The more you trust your own instincts, the better you'll like the finished design. In stitching the little finch on page 32, for example, I tried to portray the way this perky little bird makes me feel, rather than striving to capture each feather in exact detail. It's the idea of a bird in hand that gives this design appeal, not ornithological accuracy. The popular portraitist John Brewster, Jr. (who painted the *Boy with Finch* at left around 1880), may never have sketched a bird in the wild, as John J. Audubon did, but Mr. Brewster's little finch fairly bursts with song all the same. I followed his lead.

$\mathcal{W}$HEN I LOOKED UP *FINCH* IN THE DICTIONARY, I FOUND THE description of a small bird with stout build and short beak, that "is often colorful and sometimes a fine singer." There are lots of different kinds of

finches, and though there is always a chorus of finches outside my studio windows from early spring on, I can't tell you exactly which sort of finch this needlepoint fellow might be. I do know that he has a pleasing shape and is very colorful indeed. I'm also convinced that he's a fine singer.

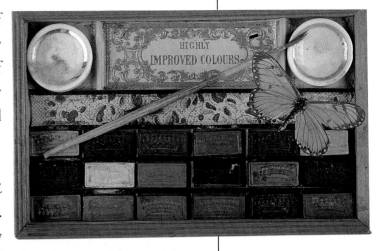

*E*VOCATIVE SHAPE AND SIMPLICITY OF LINE are as important as color in folk art designs. Parading across the bottom of the page are tiny carved birds, once part of the Christmas village display that stood beneath the tree of my mother's childhood friends. Their simple shapes and now-faded colors say "birds" to me as surely as any Audubon painting.

*F*OLK ARTISTS, OF COURSE, WERE NOT THE ONLY PAINTERS TO take a bold approach to color. While stitching these designs, I made repeated pilgrimages to a Matisse show at the Museum of Modern Art in New York City. His brilliant, no-holds-barred way with color fairly took my breath away, and inspired a more daring color mix in my own needle paintings. For any artist, this kind of cross-fertilization is one of life's happy accidents. Keep your heart receptive and your eyes open, and everything you see will inform your work. Whenever I'm stuck, I find that if I take a walk and look around me, something will always click and get me pointed in a new direction.

ALTHOUGH I PUSH FOR VIBRANT COLOR AND STARTLING CONTRAST IN MY OWN DESIGNS, YOU MIGHT WANT TO PLAY WITH THE SOFTER SHADES AND SUBTLER PALETTE OF A WATER-COLOR SKETCH IN YOURS. JUST FOLLOW YOUR HEART!

SQUIRRELS ARE A FAMILIAR part of my neighborhood landscape in New York's Greenwich Village, and I couldn't resist including one in this collection. No timid little gray squirrels for me, however. Our urban squirrels are streetwise and utterly fearless; given half a chance, they'll eat from your hand—or from any other surface that stands still for more than a minute! I wanted to capture that sassy, self-confident image in my portrait, so I stitched the little fellow's fur in mottled blues and gave him a bushy, golden yellow tail. Set against a background of brilliant scarlet, that tail stands out like a signal flag, proclaiming "Hey! Here I am, look at me!"

THIS WAS THE FIRST—BUT NOT THE LAST—DESIGN THAT CAUSED me to question my original decision to create only designs of hands holding objects for this collection. The initial version of the squirrel, with hand included, struck me as somewhat static, and the hand seemed awkward. I stitched a first version of the medallion design into a plump little pincushion (pictured on page 33), but finally decided that my squirrel might be happier perched on his oak bough all by himself. A second version of the design, sans hand, is mounted on the mahogany footstool, right.

THE SQUIRREL IS AN EXCELLENT EXAMPLE OF HOW ONE PORTION of a design often dictates the whole. Let the design evolve: You don't have to stick stubbornly to your first idea. If you're not happy with what you've sketched or stitched, try isolating each element; save the parts that please you and discard the rest. You have to be ruthless with any design—pruning and grafting elements until it feels just *right*.

$\mathcal{E}$VERYONE ADORES BUTTERFLIES. WITH THEIR SIMPLE shapes and improbable hues, each one is like a little piece of folk art on the wing. Real butterflies come in every imaginable color scheme—should we be satisfied with anything less in stitchery?

$\mathcal{C}$HILDREN, ESPECIALLY, ARE CHARMED BY BUTTER-flies and eagerly reach for any crayon or paintpot in sight to get them down on paper. Theirs is a playful approach to art we'd all do well to emulate. Indeed, Picasso himself (a consummate sophisticate who cherished the childlike in art) once said: *"Quand je n'ai pas de bleu, je mets de rouge"*; "When I haven't any blue, I just use some red." Though I can't swear to the accuracy of the quote (which I found on a French T-shirt), I love the idea of mixing colors as fancy dictates.

$\mathcal{I}$ RARELY INVEST MY STITCHERIES WITH A "MESSAGE," BUT this one is a sure signal that we can all break free of conventional boundaries if we just give it a whirl. I had great fun choosing colors for the butterfly itself, but the background and border colors caused me no end of trouble. Caribbean Blue was jazzy enough for the background, but curiously it still seemed flat until I stuck in some stripes in a slightly darker shade of the same blue to give it depth and movement. Here again, I cribbed from my folk art mentors, who often used stripes or subtly patterned backgrounds to enliven their paintings.

$\mathcal{E}$MBOLDENED, I ADDED A FEW ROWS OF CHARTREUSE (a color I *hate*) and a border of turquoise, and the design took wing. I haven't decided yet whether this particular butterfly is settling in for a landing or taking off in flight—but then, I often feel that way myself!

THE BUTTERFLY DESIGN WAS LIKE A BLACK AND WHITE PICTURE JUST WAITING TO BE COLORED IN, AN OPEN INVITATION TO EXPLORE ALL THE COLORS IN NATURE'S REPERTOIRE (SEE PAPER STICKERS BELOW)—AND A FEW OF MY OWN INVENTION (SEE SKETCH ABOVE).

*F*OR ALL OF THE DESIGNS IN *A SHOW OF HANDS,* WITH their simple shapes, decorative patterns, and relatively limited palettes, color takes on tremendous importance. I wanted each picture to be beautiful, but above all, I wanted it to be bold, lively, eye-catching; in a word, *fun*. I pushed for brilliance, contrast, intensity, and wit, and in so doing found myself taking chances with color in ways I'd never done before. Some of my experiments were disastrous, but the exhilaration when everything finally came together was absolutely delicious.

*W*ORKING WITH THE INTENSE HUES I FAVORED for these sewings, I had to toss all my painterly notions of color out the window. Even for an experienced stitcher, the only sure way to test out a color combination is to stitch it on canvas and see how it works. This requires lots of trial and error, lots of stitching in and ripping out, but if you view these experiments as an integral part of the design process, you'll learn something new and valuable from every stitch and every rip. If you stick with it, trust your instincts, push just a little bit further to get exactly what you want, the result will be a splendid triumph, a uniquely personal design that will cheer your heart long after the stitching is done.

*O*NE MORE PIECE OF ADVICE: DON'T JUST STICK TO COLORS you *like*. One of the most interesting things about needlepoint is the totally unexpected effect certain colors of yarn have when worked together. Often, when I am at my wits' end trying to make a design work, I find that a line or two of the most unlikely color—a color I would never wear or paint on my walls or even use to wrap the garbage, a color that sets my teeth on edge—is the very color I need to bring the design into focus.

THE PATTERNS

WHAT YOU'LL NEED

◆ 18 x 18-INCH SQUARE OF NO. 12 MONO CANVAS.

◆ NO. 20 TAPESTRY NEEDLE.

◆ 3-STRAND PATERNAYAN PERSIAN WOOL OR OTHER NEEDLEPOINT YARN IN THE FOLLOWING COLORS AND APPROXIMATE AMOUNTS:

No.	Color	Yds.
262	Cream	7
321	Med. Plum	3
322	Lt. Plum	3
443	Golden Brown	3
445	Lt. Golden Brown	3
471	Toast Brown	6
491	Lt. Flesh	5
493	Med. Flesh	5
500	Dk. Federal Blue	3
502	Med. Federal Blue	4
574	Turquoise	1
661	Pine Green	135
712	Mustard	2
733	Honey Gold	3
861	Dk. Copper	2
862	Med. Copper	2
863	Lt. Copper	4
912	Dusty Pink	12
930	Rusty Rose	110

THE FINCH

𝒯o CREATE THE 14 x 14-INCH DESIGN PICTURED ON PAGE 32, prepare an 18x18-inch piece of number 12 mono canvas following instructions in Chapter Six. Bind the edges of the canvas with masking tape and sketch in the design with permanent needlepoint markers to match yarn colors. Use two strands of yarn to stitch the design.

ℛEFERRING TO THE CHARTED PATTERN AND ACCOMPANYING color code, first outline the hand, cuff, and bird in continental stitch. Complete the central elements of the design in basketweave.

𝒩EXT, MEASURE OFF AND STITCH IN THE INNER BORDER OF THE design in Dusty Pink. Fill in the background square in Pine Green basketweave stitch. Finally, plot out the border, stitch in Rusty Rose ground, and fill in with Pine Green dots. To finish, consult Chapter Six.

262	321	322	443	445	471	491

493	500	502	574	661	712	733

861	862	863	912	930

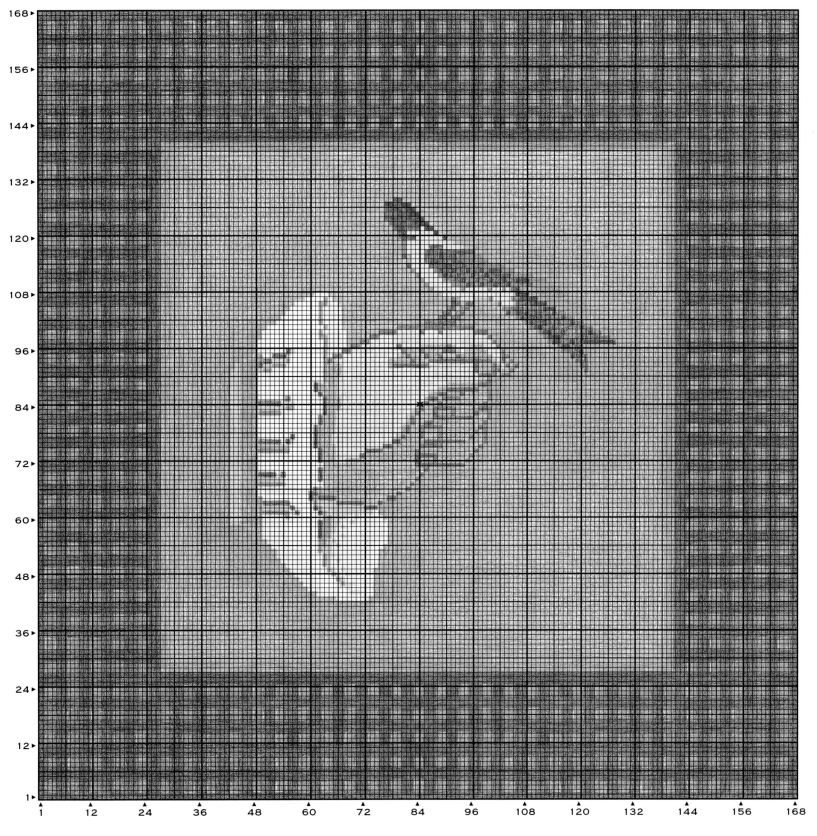

✕ MIDDLE POINT

WHAT YOU'LL NEED

◆ 18 x 18-INCH SQUARE OF NO. 12 MONO CANVAS.
◆ NO. 20 TAPESTRY NEEDLE.
◆ 3-STRAND PATERNAYAN PERSIAN WOOL OR OTHER NEEDLEPOINT YARN IN THE FOLLOWING COLORS AND APPROXIMATE AMOUNTS:

No.	Color	Yds.
220	Black	120
323	Plum	1
495	Dk. Wicker Brown	4
496	Med. Wicker Brown	4
500	Federal Blue	3
511	Med. Old Blue	6
544	Cobalt Blue	6
550	Dk. Ice Blue	30
551	Med. Ice Blue	85
602	Dk. Forest Green	3
603	Med. Forest Green	3
690	Loden Green	3
721	Autumn Yellow	4
733	Honey Gold	27
741	Tobacco	24
863	Copper	3
940	Cranberry	24

THE SQUIRREL

To CREATE THE 14 x 14-INCH DESIGN PICTURED ON PAGE 33, prepare an 18 x 18-inch piece of number 12 mono canvas following instructions in Chapter Six. Bind the edges of the canvas with masking tape and sketch in the design with permanent needlepoint markers to match yarn colors. Use two strands of yarn to stitch the design.

REFERRING TO THE CHARTED PATTERN AND ACCOMPANYING color code, first outline the hand and cuff in continental stitch, then fill in with basketweave. Next, work the stem, leaves, and acorns, then work the squirrel. Don't worry if your stitched spots don't match the chart exactly; it's the overall effect that counts. Add four short, straight stitches for the squirrel's whiskers, using a single strand of Old Blue yarn.

PLOT OUT THE MEDALLION BORDER AND STITCH, THEN complete the background in basketweave. Find the center point of one side of the medallion and begin to work the border pattern from that point out toward the edges. To stitch the squirrel without the hand, as I did for the stool on page 37, simply extend the stem and add an extra oak leaf to balance the design.

220	323	495	496	500	511	544

550	551	602	603	690	721	733

741	863	940

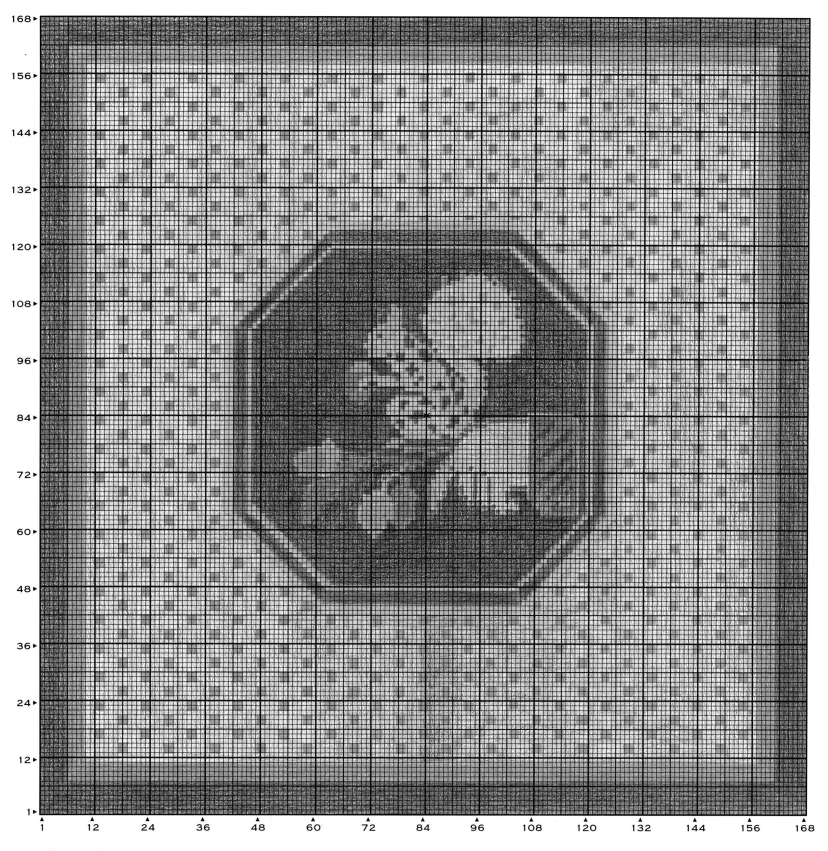

x Middle Point

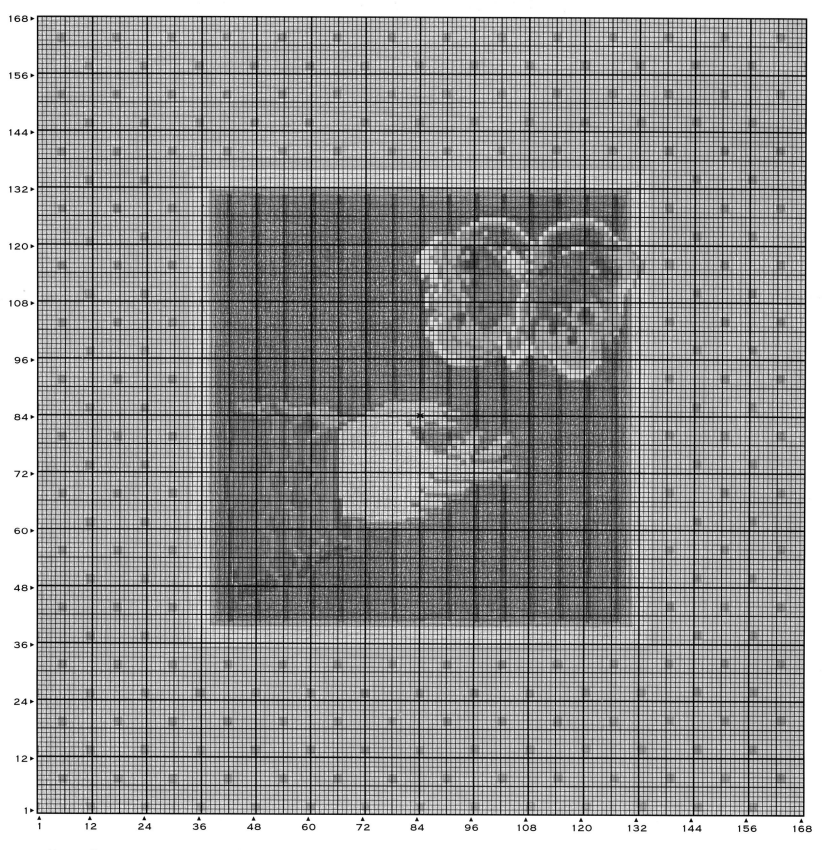

✕ MIDDLE POINT

THE BUTTERFLY

$\mathcal{T}$O CREATE THE 14 x 14-INCH DESIGN PICTURED ON PAGE 38, prepare an 18 x 18-inch square of number 12 mono canvas following instructions in Chapter Six. Bind the edges of the canvas with masking tape and sketch the design with permanent needlepoint markers to match yarn colors. Use two strands of yarn to stitch the design.

$\mathcal{R}$EFERRING TO THE CHARTED PATTERN AND ACCOMPANYING color code, first outline the hand, cuff, and butterfly in continental stitch and complete in basketweave. Plot and stitch the inner border, then carefully measure off and stitch the striped background. Work the border from the center point out toward the edges to keep the design balanced.

$\mathcal{T}$O COMPLETE THE PILLOW, REFER TO CHAPTER SIX.

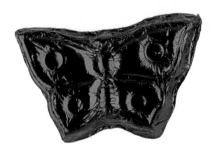  

♦ 18 x 18-INCH SQUARE OF NO. 12 MONO CANVAS.

♦ NO. 20 TAPESTRY NEEDLE.

♦ 3-STRAND PATERNAYAN PERSIAN WOOL OR OTHER NEEDLEPOINT YARN IN THE FOLLOWING COLORS AND APPROXIMATE AMOUNTS:

NO.	COLOR	YDS.
303	Med. Violet	4
304	Lt. Violet	4
332	Lavender	4
490	Flesh	5
540	Darkest Cobalt	19
541	Dk. Med. Cobalt	80
542	Med. Cobalt	65
543	Lt. Med. Cobalt	10
552	Med. Ice Blue	3
554	Lt. Ice Blue	3
591	Dk. Caribbean Blue	6
592	Med. Caribbean Blue	125
692	Med. Loden	24
693	Loden	4
863	Copper	3
902	Dk. American Beauty	2
903	Med. American Beauty	11
904	Lt. American Beauty	3

303	304	332	490	540	541
542	543	552	554	591	592
692	693	863	902	903	904

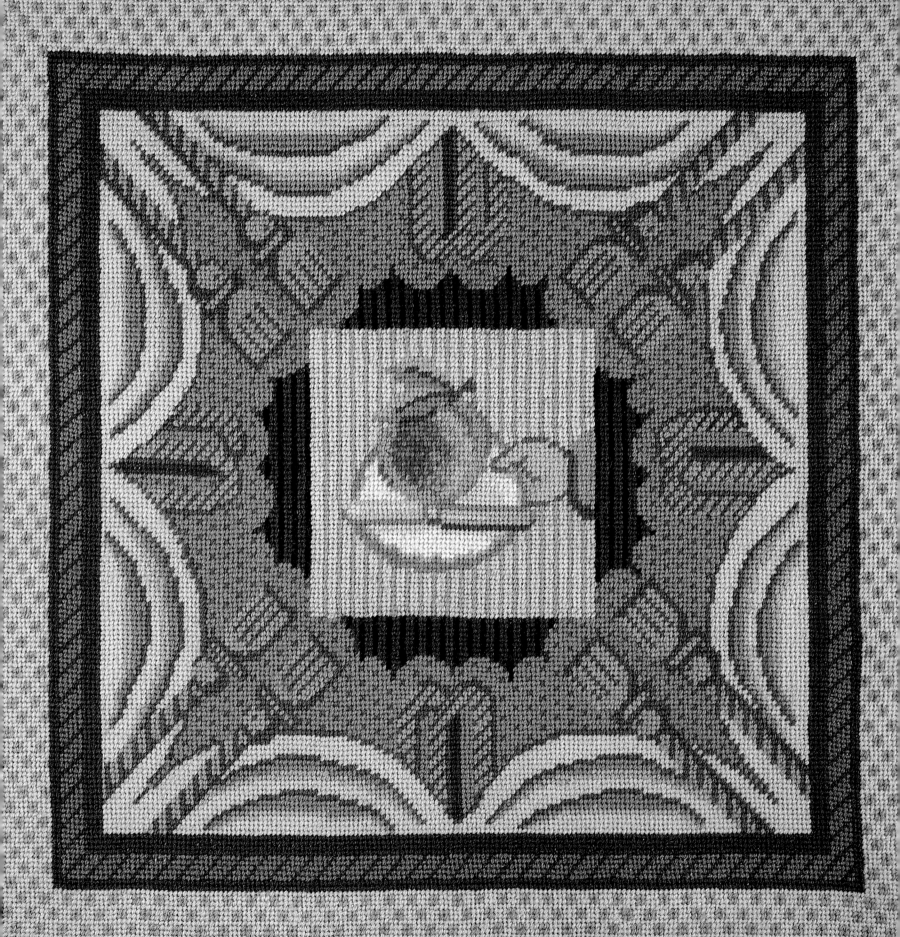

Chapter Three

THE PLEASURES OF PATTERN

*J*UST AS THE PERFECT FRAME ENHANCES ANY PAINTING, A UNIQUE BORDER CAN TRANSFORM EVEN THE SIMPLEST STITCHERY INTO A PERSONAL MASTERPIECE. LIKE SOME GIDDY IMPRESARIO, I LOVE TO CREATE THE-ATRICAL FRAMES AND TONGUE-IN-CHEEK FLOURISHES TO SHOWCASE MY DESIGN.

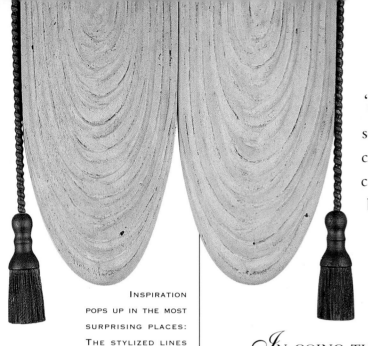

"*Showcase*" is indeed the term for the first set of projects in this chapter, because, just like raising the curtain on an empty stage, I actually sketched in the lyrically swagged and tasseled borders for this design long before I had any idea what to stitch in the center. The object was to create a single, sumptuous border that would provide the perfect setting for a changeable "cast" of motifs. I wanted a design that would draw the eye in and shout "Ta-da! Take a look at this."

In going through my research on nineteenth-century American portraits, I kept coming across tassels and curtains, curtains and tassels in the background of painting after painting. This may have been a period convention, or simply an artist's clever ploy to avoid the tedious task of portraying a patron's more complex household furnishings. (It's interesting to note that when photography became popular in the 1850s, artfully draped swags of fabric, trimmed with tassels, were often the backdrop of choice for portraits staged in the photographer's studio.)

Whatever the reason they popped up in those early paintings, I thought the swags and tassels were great fun, and I was dying to get them into some of my stitcheries. For every artist, this is the serendipitous part of design—stumbling upon an image or motif that "speaks" to you in unexpected ways. I cast my preliminary sketches in shades of gray, arranging and rearranging folds of fabric and tossing in lots of stripes and dots and scallops to

Inspiration pops up in the most surprising places: The stylized lines and weathered hue of these carved wooden curtains (salvaged from a turn-of-the-century hearse!) influenced my subdued choice of colors for the swag and tassel border. Below, pencilled sketches of some of the fruit inserts.

enliven the mix. By the time I'd added the last flourish, the frame had grown to eighteen inches square—four inches larger than other designs in the collection! Sometimes I do get carried away, but that's the charm of stitching patterns. My aim was to give the border a sense of depth and texture without relying on color for impact. I wanted to reserve color, this time, for the center motif—whatever it turned out to be. The baroquely sculpted setting called for the simplest of centerpieces. And what better foil for all this frippery, I thought, than a simple, solitary piece of fruit? Selecting the humblest of props—a blue-rimmed plate and a bone-handled knife—I busily stitched in my pièce de résistance: one perfect peach. Understudy motifs followed in quick succession: a sun-ripened pear and a Granny Smith apple—each equally worthy of star billing (pages 52-53). All three fruits were plucked from a set of antique botanical prints (left), and each bursts with color, despite its simple shape.

THE CLUSTER OF PURPLE GRAPES ON PAGE 49 IS ONE OF SEVERAL stitched motifs that didn't make the final cut in this production—but you might prefer to cast either the grapes or your own favorite fruit (or vegetable) in the starring role. Trust your own inclinations, preferences, and passions—it's the best way to put your personal stamp on any design.

To WORK THE 5 1/2 X 5 1/2-INCH CENTER MOTIFS INTO the overall design, I stitched each one onto a subtly striped background that blends nicely into the inner border of the frame. Whatever motif you choose for the center of the frame, keep the design simple and the colors bright. To create a custom frame for a specific item, you might want to play with a different palette—but I think you'll find that stitching this particular pattern in a single color family is most successful.

THOUGH I SETTLED ON MUTED GRAYS FOR MY SWAGGED BORDER, RICH SHADINGS OF THE ANTIQUE TASSELS BELOW MIGHT INSPIRE A DIFFERENT—AND EQUALLY APPEALING—COLOR SCHEME. A BIRTHDAY GIFT FROM A BELOVED FRIEND, THESE SCRUMPTIOUS TASSELS ARE MY PERSONAL GOOD LUCK CHARM.

THIS ANTIQUE LINEN
EMBROIDERER'S
POUCH, STOKED WITH
SKEINS OF SILK FLOSS
IN A DAZZLING ARRAY
OF COLORS, IS AMONG
MY MOST PRIZED POS-
SESSIONS. THE MIX OF
SHADES IS A CON-
STANT SOURCE OF
INSPIRATION WHEN I'M
WORKING ON COLOR
STUDIES FOR A NEW
DESIGN.

THOUGH WOOL YARN
DOES NOT REFLECT
LIGHT AS SILK DOES,
SIMILAR EFFECTS OF
TEXTURE AND DIMEN-
SION CAN BE
ACHIEVED WITH AN
UNEXPECTED MIX OF
COLORS—SUCH AS
THOSE I'VE USED TO
DAPPLE THE PEAR

AND THE APPLE PIC-
TURED ON THESE TWO
PAGES. STUDY BOTAN-
ICAL PRINTS AND
PAINTINGS TO DISCOVER
WHAT COLORS DIFFER-
ENT ARTISTS HAVE
USED TO GIVE LIFE
AND LUSTER TO THEIR
SUBJECTS, THEN EX-
PERIMENT WITH YARNS
TO DUPLICATE THE
EFFECTS THAT PLEASE
YOU. THE MORE YOU
PRACTICE, THE MORE
COMFORTABLE YOU'LL
BECOME WITH COLOR
MIXING, AND YOUR
CHOICES WILL BE-
COME MORE SPONTA-
NEOUS. YOU'LL QUICKLY
MOVE FROM COPYING
TO CREATING YOUR
OWN PALETTE.

𝒯o MY DELIGHT, I FOUND THAT NINETEENTH-CENTURY FOLK were almost as fond of cherries and strawberries as I am. In portraits of the period, children, in particular, often clutched small sprays of one or the other in their chubby little fists. Perhaps these clusters of fruit symbolized the promise of youth or the prosperity of the household—or perhaps the artists simply painted them in, as I have stitched them, just for the fun of it.

𝒟ESPITE MY AFFECTION FOR CHERRIES, THIS DESIGN BEDEVILED me from first sketch to final stitch. Indeed, certain of my designs, like certain characters in a novel, seem to take on a life of their own, leading me down unexpected but delightful new paths. These creative side trips may slow my progress, but they're always instructive and often exciting.

ANTIQUE BOTANICAL PRINTS, ABOVE, AND THIS CHARMING POR-TRAIT OF A GIRL HOLD-ING CHERRIES BY ROBERT LOTTRIDGE DORR, PROBABLY 1814–1815, LEFT, WERE AMONG MY SOURCES FOR THE CHERRY DESIGN.

𝒜s I BEGAN TO SKETCH, A FIRST MODEST LITTLE CLUSTER of cherries soon blossomed into a cascade of fruit and foliage. So, to balance the weight of the cherries, I first lengthened the stems, then extended the hand, and finally angled the center motif so that it broke out of the background square and spilled into the border. Next, I worried for days over the perfect shade of purple for the center square and fiddled endlessly with the width and color of the border. The interplay among all these elements is a delicate balancing act, and it takes both patience and daring—and a little luck—to get that balance exactly right. But all the work is worth it in the end. The final design has such a jauntiness, it makes my heart sing.

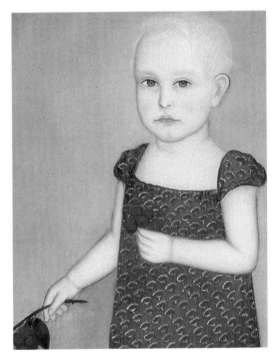

SINCE I'D RATHER DO NEEDLEPOINT THAN ALMOST ANYTHING else, there has always been a special place in my heart for the old "Curlylocks" nursery rhyme we learned as children. Its fanciful promise embodies many a stitcher's secret dream:

> *Thou shalt not wash dishes*
> *Not yet feed the swine,*
> *But sit on a cushion*
> *And sew a fine seam,*
> *And feed upon strawberries,*
> *sugar and cream.*

IS IT ANY WONDER I LOVE STRAWBERRIES SO? THERE'S A certain frivolity about this little fruit that tickles my fancy. With its absurdly dimpled berries and extravagantly detailed leaves, the strawberry is simply delicious—and I wanted to capture that feeling in needlepoint.

AMONG MY FAVORITE THINGS ARE ODDS AND ENDS OF strawberry creamware I've collected over the years—a few cups and saucers, gaily patterned plates, and a splendid old sugar bowl. They were all lined up on a table before me as I set out to sketch this design. I've always found that when you respond to a subject in a personal way, when you see with the heart rather than just with the draftsman's eye, it imparts a truth and vitality to the picture that can be achieved in no other way.

IN THIS DESIGN, ALMOST EVERY PATTERN ELEMENT STEMS FROM the strawberries themselves—even the polka dot cuff and the lively speckled border echo the seeded fruit. And note the mismatched strips of color along the inner border. I stitched them in on a whim—they seem to add just the touch of frivolity I'd been after from the very beginning.

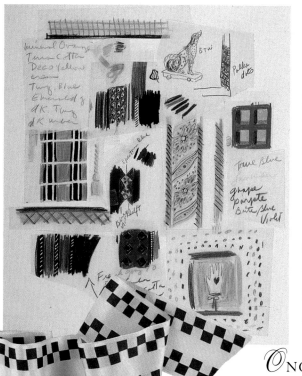

As you may have noticed, I'm crazy about borders. They're an integral part of the designs in this collection, but I almost always frame all of my needlepoint designs with a contrasting border—sometimes only a few stitches wide—just to give them a finished look.

I'm constantly on the lookout for fabric swatches and wallpaper scraps with lively patterns I can work into border designs. Plaids, of course, are special favorites, but I'm also fond of stripes and polka dots, checks and scallops and interesting little squiggles.

Once I've stitched a border pattern that pleases me, I slip a sketched or charted pattern of it into my files for future reference. Since penciled sketches never quite capture the vibrancy of finished needlepoint, I've also gotten into the habit of stitching up scraps of canvas with favorite borders or patterned backgrounds in various color combinations to stash in my files. Bookmark size, about 2 x 6 inches, is large enough to give a good sense of the overall pattern. These strips can then be pinned up beside a work in progress to judge the effect of a particular border pattern or color combination without having to actually stitch it in (and perhaps tear it out again) as the overall design evolves. Of course, this little trick doesn't always help, but I believe in taking shortcuts whenever possible.

Leafing through A SHOW OF HANDS, you'll discover that I've used several of the border patterns to frame more than one design. The colors, and occasionally the proportions, may vary, but a well-designed border can always be recycled!

I'M ALWAYS DOODLING BORDER DESIGNS CULLED FROM FABRICS, TILES, WALLPAPERS—FROM ANYWHERE AND EVERYWHERE—IN MY SKETCHBOOK (SAMPLE PAGE ABOVE). WOVEN RIBBONS AND GEOMETRIC QUILT DESIGNS (BELOW) ALSO TRANSLATE WELL INTO NEEDLEPOINT BORDERS.

THE PATTERNS

◆ 22 x 22-INCH SQUARE
OF NO. 12 MONO CANVAS.
◆ No. 20 TAPESTRY NEEDLE.
◆ 3-STRAND PATERNAYAN
PERSIAN WOOL OR OTHER
NEEDLEPOINT YARN IN
THE FOLLOWING COLORS AND
APPROXIMATE AMOUNTS:

No.	Color	Yds.
FOR PEACH INSERT:		
203	Steel Gray	15
212	Med. Pearl Gray	3
213	Lt. Pearl Gray	1
246	Neutral Gray	40
256	Warm Gray	2
260	White	4
262	Cream	1
304	Violet	1
322	Plum	1
443	Golden Brown	1
445	Lt. Golden Brown	1
491	Med. Flesh	1
493	Lt. Flesh	2
544	Cobalt Blue	1
576	Turquoise	1
578	Lt. Turquoise	1
584	Sky Blue	3
586	Lt. Sky Blue	2
662	Pine Green	2
726	Autumn Yellow	2
727	Lt. Autumn Yellow	2
731	Honey Gold	1
863	Copper	1
934	Rusty Rose	1
953	Strawberry	1
955	Lt. Strawberry	1

CURTAINS AND TASSELS

SINCE I GOT CARRIED AWAY WITH THE BORDERS ON THIS production, the peach design on page 48 is larger than most of the other patterns in the book. Although the center motif measures just 5 1/2 x 5 1/2 inches, the border builds it up to 18 inches square! To create the entire 18 x 18-inch design, prepare a 22 x 22-inch square of number 12 mono canvas, following instructions in Chapter Six. Use two strands of yarn to stitch the design.

CHOOSE THE PEACH INSERT (CHARTED HERE) OR SUBSTITUTE THE apple or pear (charted patterns on the following pages), and sketch in the design with permanent needlepoint markers to match yarn colors. Referring to the appropriate chart and accompanying color code, first outline the center motif in continental stitch, then complete the fruit, plate, and hand in basketweave. Next, plot and stitch the background stripes for the 5 1/2 x 5 1/2 -inch center square.

TO TACKLE THE BORDER, FIRST SKETCH IN THE MAJOR OUTLINES of the design in continental stitch, working from the center of the pattern out toward the edges. If you get the basic lines of the scallops, swags, and tassels in position, the rest will fall into place.

203 212 213 246

256 260 262 304 322

443 445 491 493 544 576

578 584 586 662 726 727

731 863 934 953 955

200 201

202 203

211 212

213 221

246 256

No.	Color	Yds.
FOR SWAGGED BORDER:		
200	Darkest Steel Gray	80
201	Dk. Steel Gray	55
202	Med. Steel Gray	45
203	Lt. Steel Gray	125
211	Dk. Pearl Gray	28
212	Med. Pearl Gray	50
213	Lt. Pearl Gray	24
221	Charcoal Gray	11
246	Neutral Gray	75
256	Warm Gray	55

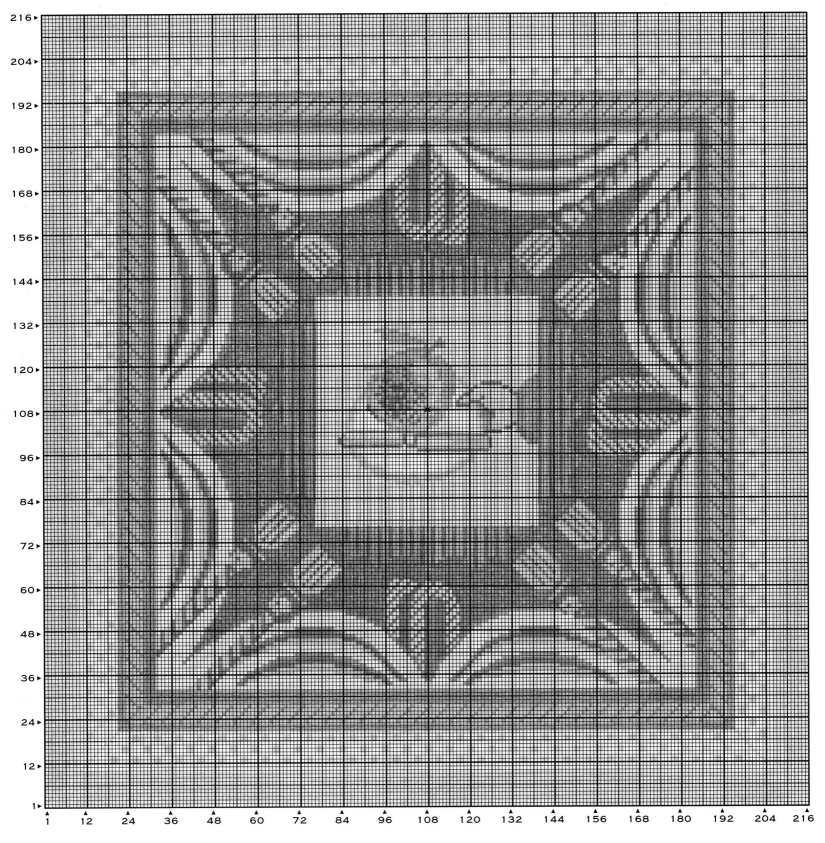

x MIDDLE POINT

WHAT YOU'LL NEED

◆ 7 1/2 x 7 1/2-INCH SQUARE OF NO. 12 MONO CANVAS (FOR THE INSERT ALONE).

◆ NO. 20 TAPESTRY NEEDLE.

◆ 3-STRAND PATERNAYAN PERSIAN WOOL OR OTHER NEEDLEPOINT YARN IN THE FOLLOWING COLORS AND APPROXIMATE AMOUNTS:

NO.	COLOR	YDS.
203	Steel Gray	15
212	Pearl Gray	2
213	Lt. Pearl Gray	1
246	Neutral Gray	40
256	Warm Gray	2
260	White	2
262	Cream	1
322	Plum	1
354	Fuchsia	1
443	Med. Golden Brown	1
445	Golden Brown	1
491	Med. Flesh	1
493	Lt. Flesh	1
575	Med. Turquoise	1
578	Lt. Turquoise	1
584	Med. Sky Blue	4
586	Lt. Sky Blue	2
698	Lt. Xmas Green	1
713	Med. Mustard	3
724	Med. Autumn Yellow	3
726	Lt. Autumn Yellow	3
741	Tobacco	1
762	Daffodil	2
863	Copper	1
907	American Beauty	1

REFER TO INSTRUCTIONS FOR "CURTAINS AND TASSELS" ON PAGE 60.

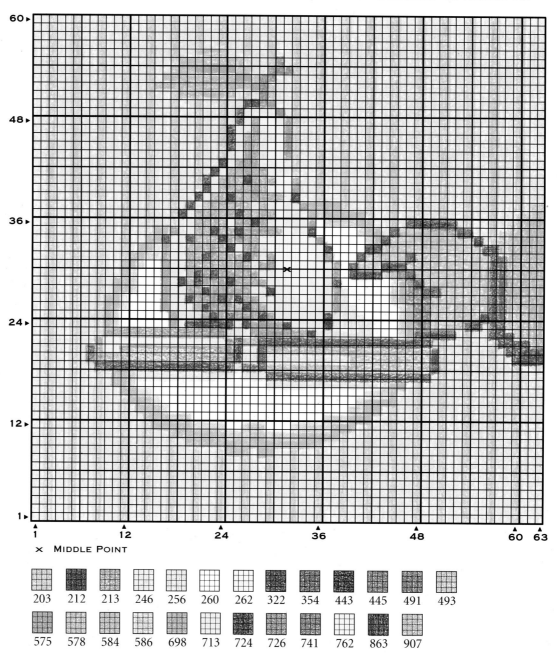

✕ MIDDLE POINT

203 212 213 246 256 260 262 322 354 443 445 491 493

575 578 584 586 698 713 724 726 741 762 863 907

APPLE INSERT

Refer to instructions for "Curtains and Tassels" on page 60.

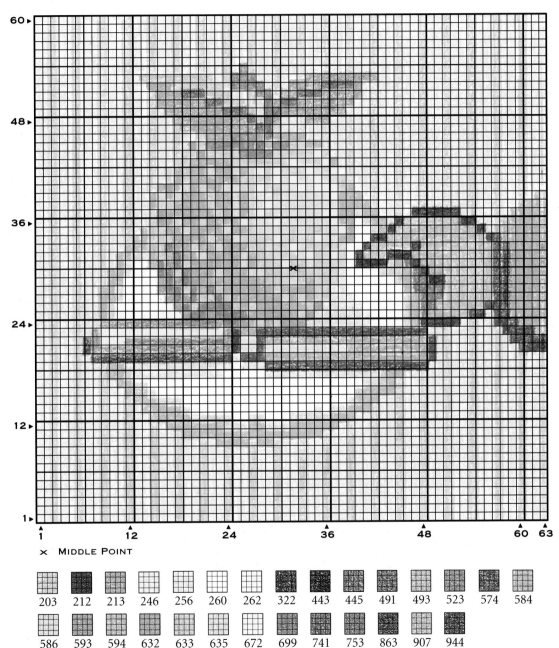

⋈ MIDDLE POINT

| 203 | 212 | 213 | 246 | 256 | 260 | 262 | 322 | 443 | 445 | 491 | 493 | 523 | 574 | 584 |

| 586 | 593 | 594 | 632 | 633 | 635 | 672 | 699 | 741 | 753 | 863 | 907 | 944 |

WHAT YOU'LL NEED

◆ SEE PAGE 62.

No.	Color	Yds.
203	Steel Gray	15
212	Pearl Gray	2
213	Lightest Pearl Gray	1
246	Neutral Gray	40
256	Warm Gray	2
260	White	2
262	Cream	1
322	Plum	2
443	Med. Golden Brown	1
445	Lt. Golden Brown	1
491	Med. Flesh	1
493	Lt. Flesh	2
523	Teal Blue	1
574	Turquoise	1
584	Med. Sky Blue	4
586	Lt. Sky Blue	2
593	Med. Caribbean Blue	3
594	Lt. Caribbean Blue	1
632	Med. Spring Green	3
633	Spring Green	3
635	Lt. Spring Green	3
672	Lime Green	2
699	Xmas Green	1
741	Tobacco	1
753	Old Gold	1
863	Copper	1
907	Lt. Amer. Beauty	1
944	Cranberry	1

WHAT YOU'LL NEED

◆ 18 x 18-INCH SQUARE OF NO. 12 MONO CANVAS.

◆ No. 20 TAPESTRY NEEDLE.

◆ 3-STRAND PATERNAYAN PERSIAN WOOL OR OTHER NEEDLEPOOINT YARN IN THE FOLLOWING COLORS AND APPROXIMATE AMOUNTS:

No.	COLOR	YDS.
310	Dk. Grape	2
311	Med. Grape	75
312	Lt. Grape	35
482	Terracotta	2
490	Med. Flesh	8
512	Dk. Old Blue	2
513	Med. Old Blue	5
520	Dk. Teal Blue	3
522	Med. Teal Blue	4
541	Cobalt Blue	11
602	Med. Forest Green	3
610	Dk. Hunter Green	3
612	Med. Hunter Green	3
753	Lt. Old Gold	1
863	Med. Copper	4
871	Rust	80
900	Darkest American Beauty	5
902	Dk. American Beauty	6
903	Med. American Beauty	5
904	Lt. American Beauty	4
912	Med. Dusty Pink	1
969	Christmas Red	5

𝒯O CREATE THE 14 x 14-INCH PILLOW PICTURED ON PAGE 54, PREPARE an 18 x 18-inch piece of number 12 mono canvas following instructions in Chapter Six. Bind the edges of the canvas with masking tape and sketch in the design with permanent needlepoint markers to match yarn colors. Use two strands of yarn to stitch the design.

𝓡EFERRING TO THE CHARTED PATTERN AND ACCOMPANYING color code, first outline the hand and cuff in continental stitch. Then stitch in the stripes on the cuff.

𝒩EXT, FILL IN THE CUFF AND HAND in basketweave stitch. Outline and fill in the cherries and leaves. Finally, fill in the Light Grape background, Cobalt inner border, and plaid outer border in basketweave stitch. (Hint: You may find it easiest to work the Grape grid on the border first, then fill in blocks of Rust afterward.) To complete the pillow, refer to details on finishing in Chapter Six.

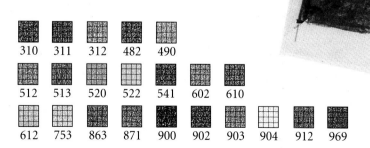

310 311 312 482 490

512 513 520 522 541 602 610

612 753 863 871 900 902 903 904 912 969

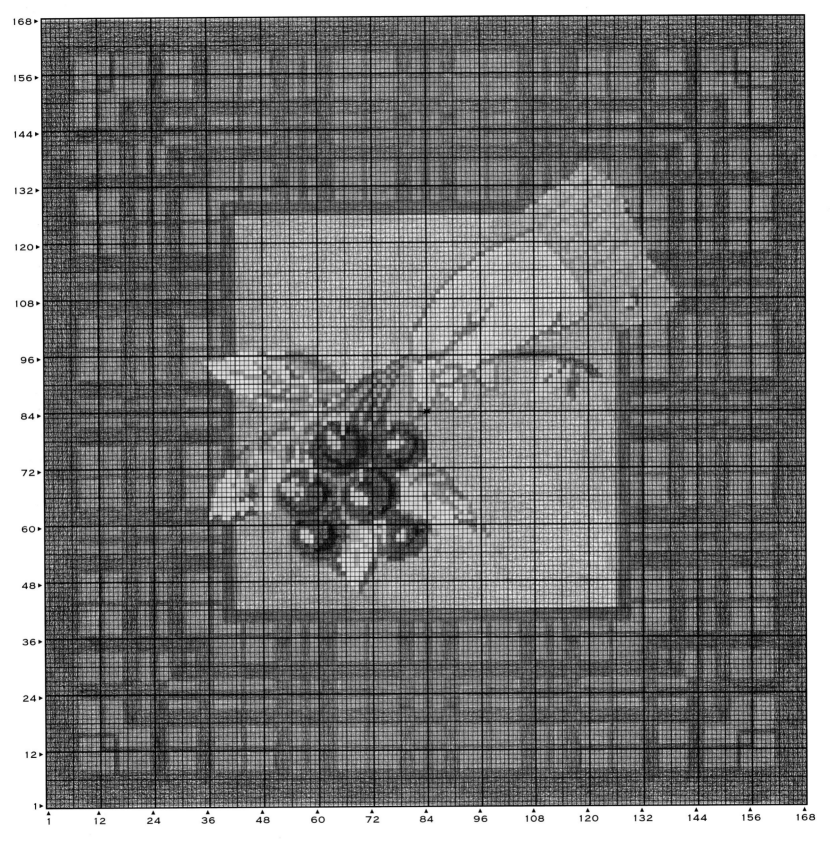

× MIDDLE POINT

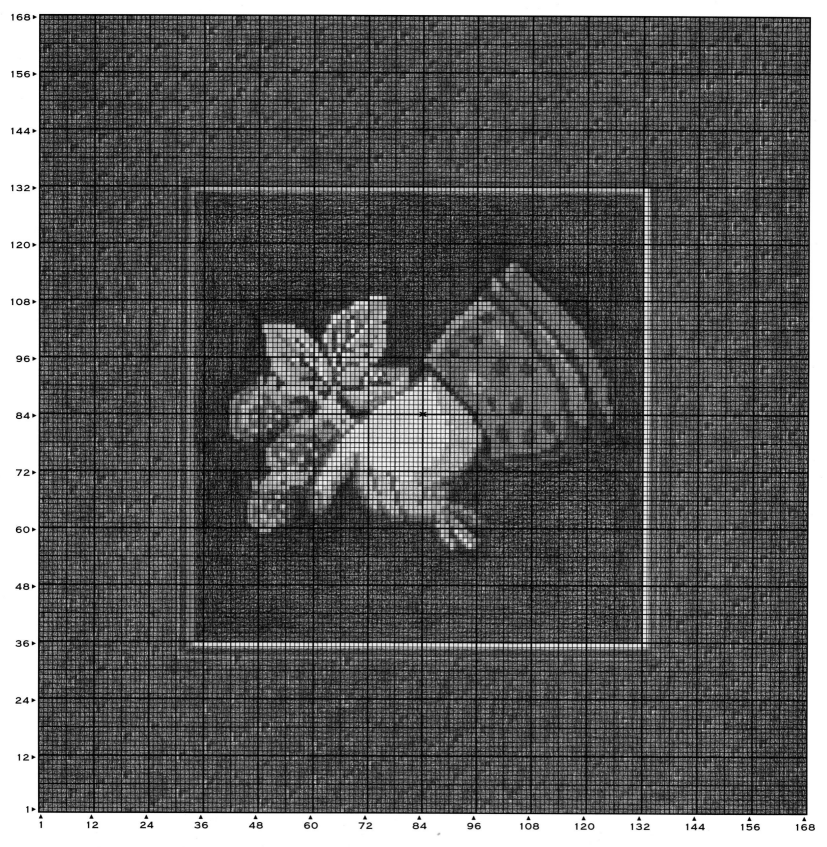

✕ MIDDLE POINT

STRAWBERRIES

$\mathcal{T}$O CREATE THE 14×14-INCH STRAWBERRY PICTURE ON PAGE 57, prepare an 18×18-inch piece of number 12 mono canvas following instructions in Chapter Six. Bind the edges of the canvas with masking tape and sketch in the design with permanent needlepoint markers to match yarn colors. Use two strands of yarn to stitch the design.

$\mathcal{R}$EFERRING TO THE CHARTED PATTERN AND ACCOMPANYING color code, first outline the hand and cuff in continental stitch. Fill in the stripes and polka dots on the cuff, then complete the hand and cuff in basketweave.

$\mathcal{N}$EXT, OUTLINE AND STITCH IN THE STRAWBERRIES AND LEAVES. Plot and stitch in the multicolored inner border, then complete the Dark Brown background in basketweave. Work the outer seeded border in Dark Christmas Red and add Navy Blue dots. To complete, see details on finishing in Chapter Six.

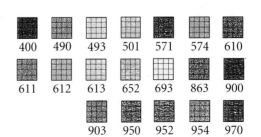

400	490	493	501	571	574	610
611	612	613	652	693	863	900
	903	950	952	954	970	

WHAT YOU'LL NEED

◆ 18×18-INCH SQUARE OF NO. 12 MONO CANVAS.

◆ NO. 20 TAPESTRY NEEDLE.

◆ 3-STRAND PATERNAYAN PERSIAN WOOL OR OTHER NEEDLEPOINT YARN IN THE FOLLOWING COLORS AND APPROXIMATE AMOUNTS:

No.	Color	Yds.
400	Dk. Brown	40
490	Med. Flesh	3
493	Pale Flesh	4
501	Med. Federal Blue	2
571	Navy Blue	35
574	Dk. Turquoise	6
610	Darkest Hunter Green	5
611	Dk. Hunter Green	8
612	Med. Hunter Green	8
613	Lt. Hunter Green	9
652	Med. Olive Green	3
693	Med. Loden Green	5
863	Copper	3
900	Darkest American Beauty	6
903	Med. American Beauty	4
950	Dk. Strawberry	2
952	Med. Strawberry	2
954	Lt. Strawberry	2
970	Dk. Christmas Red	145

Chapter Four

TELLING DETAILS

NOVICE WRITERS ARE OFTEN
ADVISED TO WRITE ABOUT WHAT
THEY KNOW BEST AND LOVE MOST, AND
THE SAME HOLDS TRUE FOR ARTISTS IN
ANY FIELD. HERE, I'VE SELECTED AN
ASSORTMENT OF CHILDHOOD TREASURES
TO PORTRAY IN NEEDLEPOINT, STITCHING
IN THE SPIRITED COLORS AND QUIRKY
DETAILS THAT MAKE ME SMILE.

THE CIRCUS FIG-
URES PICTURED
HERE PROVIDE
L I V E L Y
INSPIRA-
TION FOR
NEEDLE-
P O I N T
PICTURES.
T H O U G H
MY NEEDLE-
POINT DOLL STANDS
FOURSQUARE IN HER
STITCHERY PORTRAIT,
THE ANTIC POSES
OF THESE ANTIQUE
CLOWN FIGURES SUG-
GEST WHOLE NEW
DESIGN POSSIBILITIES.

$\mathscr{E}$VERY PICTURE, PAINTED OR STITCHED, HAS a story to tell, and it is in the personal details you add to the picture that that story is most truly told. The natural world is an endless source of inspiration for needlepoint, as I illustrated in the first three chapters of this book. But personal mementos offer a wonderfully rich source of design ideas as well.

$\mathscr{L}$IKE MANY OF YOU, I HAVE AN ABIDING AFFECTION FOR THE oft-used and well-loved objects in my life. Childhood treasures in particu-lar—mine or someone else's—have an instant claim upon my heart. Perhaps the knowledge that something has been cherished in the past, that even the most raggedy doll or moth-eaten animal was the dearest compan-ion of a real child in days gone by, gives that toy a special appeal. Though the paint be chipped or the costume frayed, such toys are filled with life, and their stories, real or imagined, are a joy to translate into stitchery. In my mind and with my needle, I repair the damaged parts, restore the vivid colors of childhood's memory, and stitch them up as they first appeared to me when both toys and I were young.

$\mathscr{T}$HE COSTUMED POPPET ON PAGE 68 THAT OPENS THIS chapter might be a composite portrait of every doll I ever had—or longed to have—as a child. One of my favorite pastimes as a little girl was to cut figures out of maga-zines, mount them on cardboard, and create fanciful finery for each one out of scraps of paper and fabric. Stitching in the puffed sleeves, the beribboned skirt, and the frilled pantaloons on this needlepoint doll brought back all the delight of those early forays into the world of haute couture .

$\mathscr{H}$OWEVER, AS IS OFTEN THE CASE AS A DESIGN evolves, my doll took on a life of her own. No matter how many

A SHOW OF HANDS

times I tried to slip a hand around her waist or beneath her feet, she seemed to want to stand on her own, and I finally had to let her do it! Still, I had become much too fond of this independent young lady to keep her out of the show—so I beg you to imagine that the hand in question has just been snatched off stage for a moment, perhaps in search of more buttons and bows to trim milady's dress.

𝒯HE FROTHY CONFECTION OF RIBBONS AND BOWS IN THE border may be my favorite part of this whole design, and the giddy mix of dots and swirls and stripes in the pattern recalls every party dress I ever loved as a child. These are the sort of personal details that give any design life and resonance.

𝒫LUCKED FROM HER RIBBON FRAME AND STITCHED ONTO THE dainty little purse on page 69, the doll still has a flirtatious air that makes me smile. Either pillow or purse would make a delightful gift for a special girl of your acquaintance.

THE ANIMALS I PICKED FOR MY PULL-TOY DESIGNS ON THE FOLLOWING PAGES ARE ALL OF THE DOMESTIC VARIETY, BUT WILDER BEASTS— LIKE LIONS AND TIGERS AND BEARS, PERHAPS—WOULD BE A TREAT TO STITCH AS WELL.

𝒥 CHOOSE A TRIO OF FAMILIAR PETS FOR THE SERIES OF needlepointed pull toys on the following pages. Other favorite childhood animals might figure in your own designs. The jaunty clowns, dashing ringmaster, and fearsome toy tiger pictured here would all translate well into stitchery, while the dear billy goat gruff at left might inspire the first of a series of farm animal stitcheries. Think of yourself as the magic fairy in Margery Williams's classic tale, *The Velveteen Rabbit*. "I take care of all the playthings that the children have loved,"she confides. "When they are old and worn out and the children don't need them any more, then I come and take them away with me and turn them into Real." Our happy task might be to turn such treasures into needlepoint instead.

A TRIO OF PULL-TOY DESIGNS—THE ORANGE CAT AND SPOTTED dog pictured here, and the speckled rooster on the following page—are three of my happiest creations.

THOUGH CHILDREN WERE OFTEN PICTURED HOLDING TOY animals of one sort or another in the folk art portraits I've seen, I don't recall any picture of a toy exactly like one of these. However, knowledgeable collectors assure me that cast iron animals and plush pull toys were as popular with children in the nineteenth century as their counterparts are with kids today. I sketched all sorts of toys from the antique samples, but settled on these three because they tickled my fancy.

ALTHOUGH I DIDN'T SET OUT TO STITCH THESE PULL TOYS AS A set, all three ended up having a number of details in common. First, each animal has a piebald coat, inspired by the richly mottled clay marbles that kids played with in days gone by, like those at left. I confined myself to two or three colors each for the cat and the rooster, but I went a bit dotty with the dog—there are ten different colors stitched into his spotted hide!

ANOTHER DETAIL THESE DESIGNS HAVE IN COMMON IS that each animal is set against a striped background, though the color combination is different for each, as is the width of the stripes. The same stippled border frames each design—a variation of the pattern originally developed for the strawberry design on page 57.

A NOTE ABOUT THE HANDS AND CUFFS ON THIS AND the other designs: Both are scaled to suit the size and shape of each center motif, but with a little fiddling, the cuffs and many of the hands are interchangeable. Modify the size and shape of each hand and cuff to suit the object on display, and select colors to complement the overall palette.

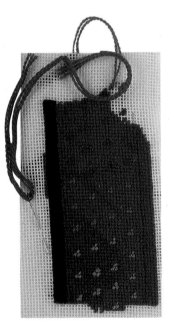

*W*ITH HIS PROUD BEARING, BRIGHT RED wattles, and spectacular plummage, this speckled rooster strutted his way right into my heart and onto the cover of a family scrapbook—a book destined to be filled with all manner of things to crow about! Outline stitches in electric blue add dimension to the design and emphasize this cocky chicken's take-charge stance.

I TRIED EVERY COLOR OF THE RAINBOW behind my rooster before finally resorting to the egg-yolk yellow you see here. It's not a color I much like on its own, but the rooster came alive when I stitched it in—so who was I to argue? Once again, I just had to follow where the design led me.

*A*LBUMS ARE BOTH A PRETTY AND A PRACTICAL WAY TO DISPLAY your needlepoint, and the choice of a cover design can be easily tailored to suit any occasion. Choose among the motifs in *A Show of Hands*, or create one of your own. Pillows and pictures are always appropriate settings, of course, but devising an imaginative way to present your needlepoint design is worth the extra effort.

*T*O COMPLETE THIS PROJECT, I BEGAN WITH A STORE-BOUGHT photo album (the kind with detachable front and back), then glued my stitchery picture onto the cover and bound the edges with chunky cording. Other designs in this collection might be mounted in the same way. (Instructions for making the album are included in Chapter Six.)

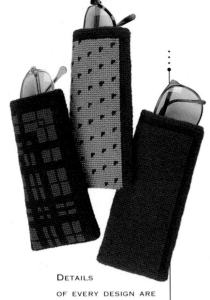

DETAILS
OF EVERY DESIGN ARE
YOURS TO MANIPULATE
AS YOU WILL. YOU
MIGHT STITCH BORDER
PATTERNS INTO GLASSES
CASES (ABOVE) OR USE
THE CAT'S HEAD
DESIGN TO PERK UP
POCKETS ON A CHILD'S
SWEATER (BELOW).
SELECT OTHER DESIGN
DETAILS TO EMBELLISH
PROJECTS OF YOUR
OWN DEVISING.

PERSONAL DETAILS ARE THE HALLMARK OF EVERY DESIGN IN this collection—the quirky choice of subjects, the combination of colors, design fillips that have special meaning to me but may be of no particular significance to anyone else. It's important, I believe, to introduce as much of the personal as possible into any handmade object. Make the most of design elements that please you and change or discard those that don't.

MANY YEARS AGO, I HAD THE GOOD FORTUNE TO HAVE A kindergarten teacher who was a splendid artist. More importantly, she was also a splendid teacher. When spring came, she would settle us all in front of our little easels, set out the paint pots and brushes, and invite us to "celebrate the season." Whatever we painted—trees and sky or flowers or friends or puddles of mud—she praised them all and always found something encouraging to say about each child's effort. She delighted in whatever was unique and individual about our pictures, and I've cherished her example from that day to this.

THERE'S ONE OTHER KIND OF PERSONAL DETAIL that I want you to keep in mind as you stitch these designs, and that is the inevitability of "mistakes." I put *mistakes* in quotes because I believe that the charm of needlepoint (or of any craft) is its handmade quality. If a finished design is a little off, slightly at variance with the original design, well, I believe that it's *supposed* to be that way. When you're following a charted pattern, there's liable to be a stitch or two out of sequence, a line that zigs a bit where it ought to zag. Just look at these "mistakes" as putting your personal stamp on my designs. Nothing could please me more.

THE PATTERNS

What You'll Need

◆ 18 x 18-inch square of no. 12 mono canvas.
◆ No. 20 tapestry needle.
◆ 3-strand Paternayan Persian wool or other needlepoint yarn in the following colors and approximate amounts:

No.	Color	Yds.
260	White	100
304	Violet	80
327	Lightest Plum	4
332	Lavender	24
340	Dk. Periwinkle	4
341	Med. Periwinkle	24
592	Med. Caribbean Blue	4
594	Lt. Caribbean Blue	6
595	Lightest Caribbean Blue	1
860	Dk. Copper	2
941	Cranberry	15
960	Darkest Hot Pink	16
961	Dk. Hot Pink	15
962	Med. Dk. Hot Pink	25
963	Med. Hot Pink	16
964	Lt. Hot Pink	12

DOLL WITH RIBBONS

*T*HERE IS NO HAND IN THE DOLL PATTERN. A GLANCE AT THE undeveloped sketch below suggests why I chose to drop the hand from my final design.

*T*O CREATE THE 14 x 14-INCH DOLL PICTURED ON PAGE 68, PREPARE an 18 x 18-inch piece of number 12 mono canvas following the instructions in Chapter Six. Bind the edges of the canvas with masking tape and sketch in the design with permanent needlepoint markers to match yarn colors. Use two strands of yarn to stitch the design.

*R*EFERRING TO THE CHARTED PATTERN AND ACCOMPANYING color code, first outline the doll in continental stitch, then fill in the details in basketweave. Plot and stitch the striped inner square. Next, plot and stitch the ribbon and bow portion of the border, before filling in the space between the ribbons and the center square. Finally, stitch the striped "ticking" design behind and beyond the ribbons. To complete the project, see details on finishing in Chapter Six. Instructions for completing the doll purse appear on page 119.

260	304	327	332	340	341

592	594	595	860	941	960

961	962	963	964

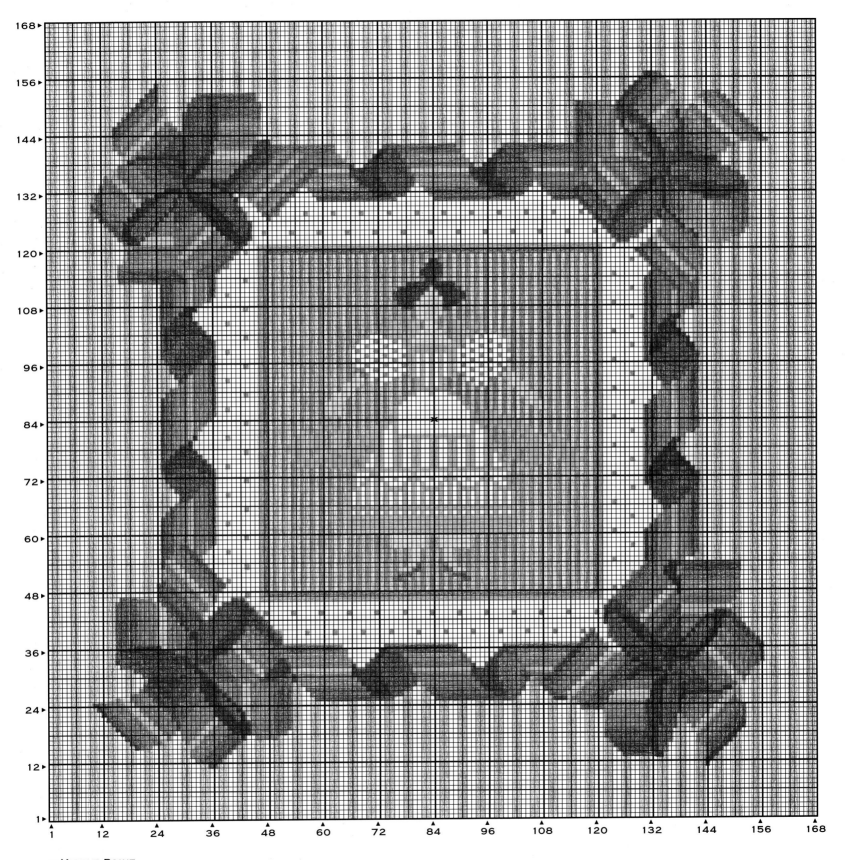

✕ MIDDLE POINT

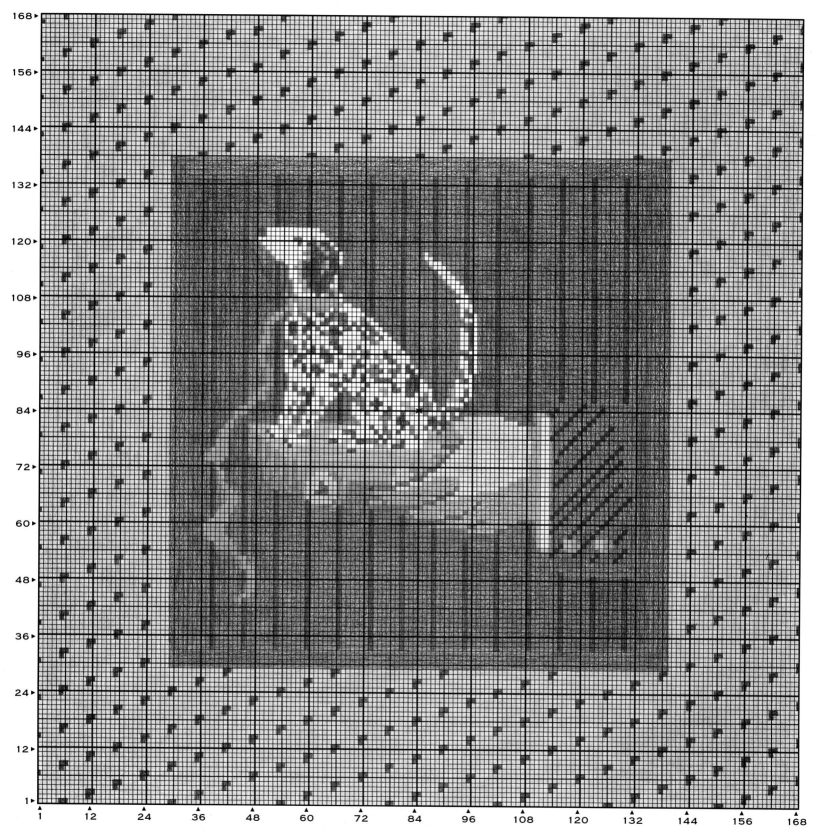

✕ MIDDLE POINT

CALICO DOG

THERE ARE TEN DIFFERENT COLORS IN THE DOG'S SPOTTED coat. If you find all those dots a bit dizzying, reduce the number of colors to three or four.

TO CREATE THE 14x14-INCH DESIGN PICTURED ON PAGE 73, prepare an 18x18-inch piece of number 12 mono canvas following instructions in Chapter Six. Bind the edges of the canvas with masking tape and sketch in the design with permanent needlepoint markers to match yarn colors. Use two strands of yarn to stitch the design.

REFERRING TO THE CHARTED PATTERN AND ACCOMPANYING color code, first outline the hand and cuff in continental stitch, then complete the motif in basketweave.

STITCH IN THE OUTLINE FOR THE DOG AND PLATFORM, THEN complete the motifs in basketweave. Don't worry if your dots don't match the pattern exactly—just sprinkle in a lively variety of spots, then fill in the background of the dog in Cream. Stitch the leash in Cobalt, then plot and stitch the inner blue border and fill in the striped background. Finally, stitch the speckled border. To add whiskers, take short, straight stitches with a single strand of yarn. See Chapter Six for tips on making a pillow.

262	313	440	490	493	540	542	570	571
621	691	693	710	715	722	732	734	760
853	863	871	900	911	930	970		

WHAT YOU'LL NEED

◆ 18 x 18-INCH SQUARE OF NO. 12 MONO CANVAS.

◆ No. 20 TAPESTRY NEEDLE.

◆ 3-STRAND PATERNAYAN PERSIAN WOOL OR OTHER NEEDLEPOINT YARN IN THE FOLLOWING COLORS AND APPROXIMATE AMOUNTS:

No.	Color	Yds.
262	Cream	7
313	Grape	2
440	Golden Brown	8
490	Lt. Flesh	4
493	Med. Flesh	4
540	Dk. Cobalt	25
542	Med. Cobalt	4
570	Dk. Navy	4
571	Navy	8
621	Shamrock Green	4
691	Dk. Loden Green	2
693	Med. Loden Green	4
710	Mustard	70
715	Lt. Mustard	3
722	Autumn Yellow	8
732	Honey Gold	7
734	Lt. Honey Gold	1
760	Daffodil	3
853	Spice	4
863	Med. Copper	3
871	Rust	4
900	American Beauty	80
911	Dusty Pink	70
930	Rusty Rose	4
970	Xmas Red	1

WHAT YOU'LL NEED

◆ 18 x 18-INCH SQUARE OF NO. 12 MONO CANVAS.

◆ NO. 20 TAPESTRY NEEDLE.

◆ 3-STRAND PATERNAYAN PERSIAN WOOL OR OTHER NEEDLEPOINT YARN IN THE FOLLOWING COLORS AND APPROXIMATE AMOUNTS:

No.	Color	Yds.
209	Pearl Gray	3
323	Med. Plum	4
324	Plum	150
325	Lt. Plum	30
490	Lt. Flesh	5
493	Med. Flesh	3
540	Dk. Cobalt	25
542	Med. Cobalt	115
561	Glacier Blue	4
701	Butterscotch	1
732	Honey Gold	6
754	Med. Old Gold	3
756	Lt. Old Gold	5
800	Dk. Marigold	8
801	Med. Marigold	2
861	Dk. Copper	5
863	Med. Copper	4
870	Rust	1
871	Med. Rust	5
952	Strawberry	2

ORANGE CAT

To CREATE THE 14 x 14-INCH DESIGN PICTURED ON PAGE 73, PREPARE an 18 x 18-inch piece of number 12 mono canvas following instructions in Chapter Six. Bind the canvas edges with masking tape and sketch in the design with permanent needlepoint markers to match yarn colors. Use two strands of yarn to stitch the design.

REFERRING TO THE CHARTED PATTERN AND ACCOMPANYING color code, first outline the hand and cuff in continental stitch, then fill in these elements in basketweave.

NEXT, STITCH THE OUTLINE FOR THE CAT AND PLATFORM, then complete the motif in basketweave. Stitch the pull cord in blue, then plot and stitch the inner border and fill in the striped background. To add whiskers, take short, straight stitches with a single strand of yarn. Finally, stitch the speckled border. Instructions for completing the pillow and for adapting the cat motif to make patch pockets (pictured on page 76) are included in Chapter Six.

209 323 324 325 490 493 540 542 561

701 732 754 756 800 801 861

863 870 871 952

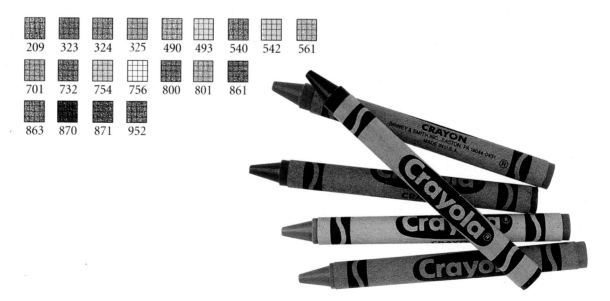

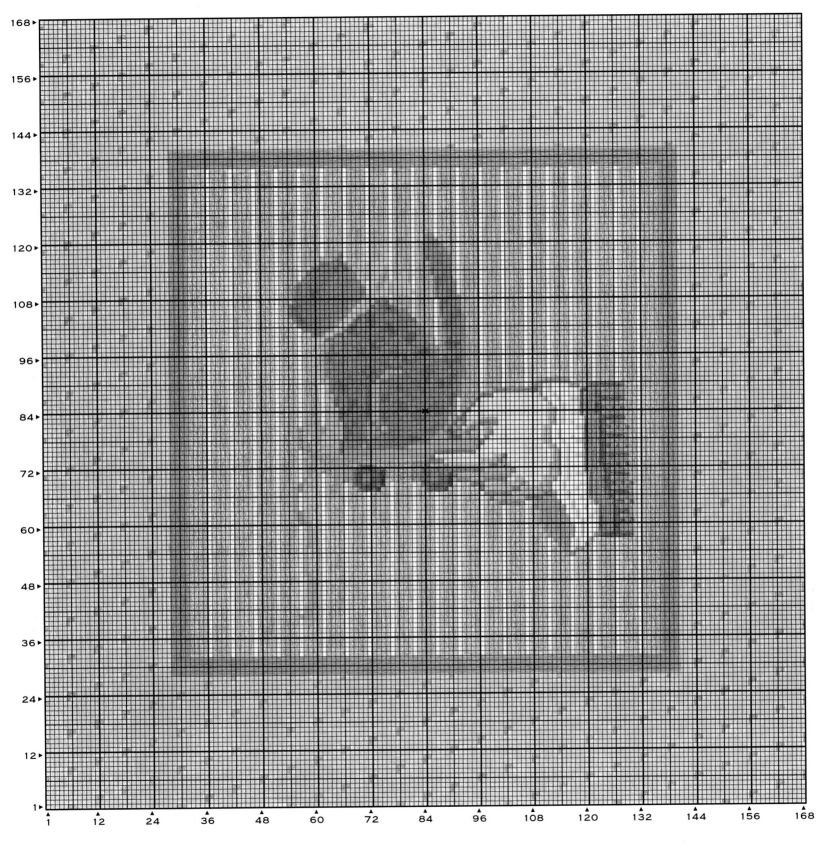

168►
156►
144►
132►
120►
108►
96►
84►
72►
60►
48►
36►
24►
12►
1►

1   12   24   36   48   60   72   84   96   108   120   132   144   156   168

✕ MIDDLE POINT

◆ 18x18-INCH SQUARE OF NO. 12 MONO CANVAS.

◆ No.20 TAPESTRY NEEDLE.

◆ 3-STRAND PATERNAYAN PERSIAN WOOL OR OTHER NEEDLEPOINT YARN IN THE FOLLOWING COLORS AND APPROXIMATE AMOUNTS:

No.	COLOR	YDS.
201	Med. Steel Gray	6
203	Lt. Steel Gray	8
262	Cream	4
491	Lt. Flesh	2
493	Med. Flesh	3
503	Federal Blue	5
511	Old Blue	3
540	Darkest Cobalt	16
541	Dk. Cobalt	110
582	Sky Blue	4
611	Hunter Green	2
612	Lt. Hunter Green	3
701	Butterscotch	2
722	Dk. Autumn Yellow	5
725	Med. Autumn Yellow	26
727	Lt. Autumn Yellow	95
863	Copper	4
970	Christmas Red	120

SPECKLED ROOSTER

$\mathcal{T}$O CREATE THE 14x14-INCH DESIGN PICTURED ON PAGE 75, prepare an 18x18-inch piece of number 12 mono canvas following instructions in Chapter Six. Bind the edges of the canvas with masking tape and sketch in the design with permanent needlepoint markers to match yarn colors. Use two strands of yarn to stitch the design.

$\mathcal{R}$EFERRING TO THE CHARTED PATTERN AND ACCOMPANYING color code, first outline the hand and cuff in continental stitch, then complete the motifs in basketweave.

$\mathcal{N}$EXT, STITCH IN THE OUTLINE FOR THE ROOSTER AND PLATFORM and complete the motifs in basketweave. Stitch in the pull cord, then plot and fill in the striped background. Finally, stitch the speckled border. Instructions for mounting the design on a purchased album cover are included in Chapter Six.

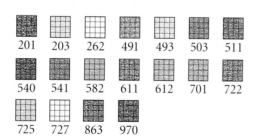

201   203   262   491   493   503   511

540   541   582   611   612   701   722

725   727   863   970

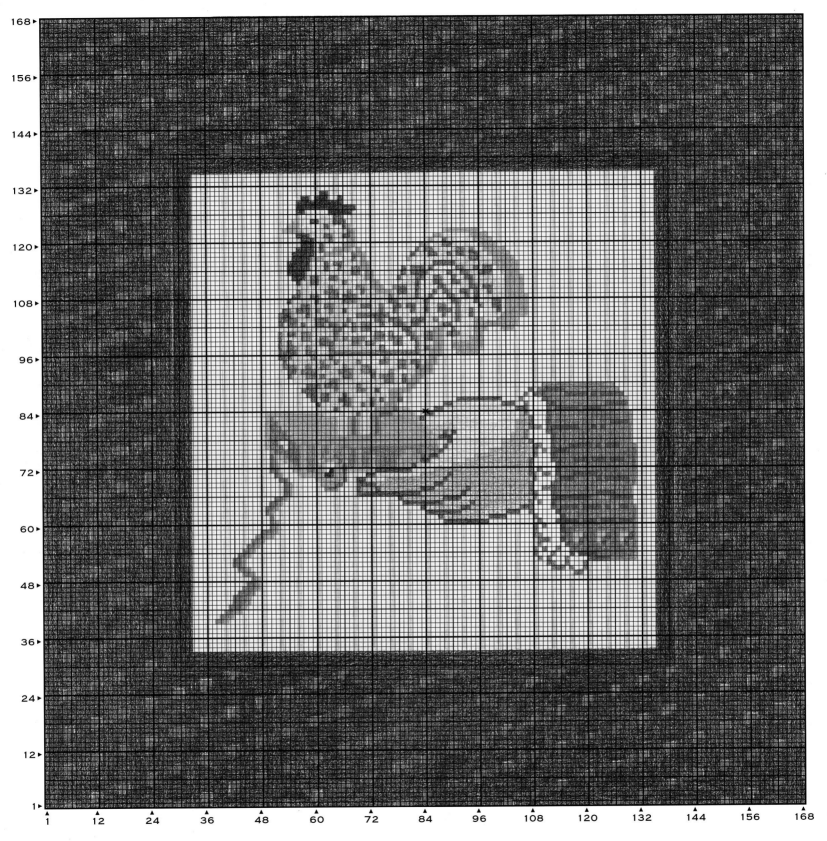

✕ Middle Point

Chapter Five

THE GIFTED HAND

FOR ME, PART OF THE PLEASURE OF HANDWORK LIES IN CREATING SOMETHING TO SHARE. IN AN AGE WHEN TIME AND EFFORT ARE PRECIOUS COMMODITIES, THERE'S A SPECIAL SATISFACTION IN GIVING SOMETHING OF BOTH—SOMETHING OF OURSELVES—TO THOSE WE LOVE. DESIGNED WITH SPECIAL FOLK IN MIND, THESE NEEDLEPOINT GIFTS ARE TRUE TOKENS OF FRIENDSHIP.

$\mathcal{I}$ FIRST LEARNED TO NEEDLEPOINT IN THE COMPANY OF MY DEAR friend Inger and have ever since thought of stitching as a sociable activity. Perfecting a design takes quiet and concentration, but once I've worked out the details of a motif and can turn my attention to filling in backgrounds and borders, there's something wonderfully soothing, almost meditative, to the rhythm of drawing the yarn in and out of the canvas.

$\mathcal{I}$N DAYS GONE BY, WHEN I SPENT TIME IN THE COUNTRY, INGER and I would often come together to stitch and talk and share a laugh. I love the idea of being able to visit with friends or sit quietly by myself and think my own thoughts—knowing that at the same time I am creating a bit of stitchery that I or someone else will use and treasure in the future. For me, this sense of time both well and pleasurably spent is part of the special appeal of needlepoint.

$\mathcal{W}$HEN I CRAFTED THE ORIGINAL DESIGN FOR A WOMAN'S hand holding a quill pen on page 86, it was with a friend—a writer—very much in mind. I wanted something specifically feminine for this design. An outrageously ruffled cuff did the trick. A hint of swags and tassles in the corner adds a touch of drama. An elegantly scripted initial personalizes the pattern—even the ring resembles one that my friend often wears.

$\mathcal{O}$NCE I'D POLISHED THIS DESIGN, I DECIDED TO ADAPT it as a petit point insert for the lid of an old-fashioned letterbox, a gift for another friend who is a prolific correspondent. Another day, as an impromptu thank you gift, I stitched up the monogrammed cardcase on page 87, combining the initial block and bits of the border pattern from the original.

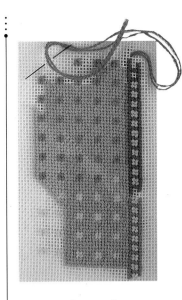

THOUGH I HADN'T PLANNED FOR IT IN MY INITIAL SKETCH (BELOW), I LOVE THE WAY THE QUILL FEATHER BREAKS OUT OF THE BACKGROUND AND INTO THE BORDER ON THIS DESIGN.

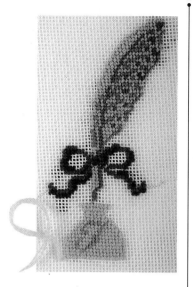

THE FIRST DESIGN FOR THIS CHAPTER WAS OF A WOMAN'S HAND holding a quill pen, but a review of my nineteenth-century portrait sources revealed that women were usually depicted with something much less assertive in hand—flowers or fans, or perhaps a book of poetry or scripture. Gentlemen, on the other hand, were frequently portrayed wielding a pen in these old folk art paintings. The pen symbolized, I suppose, the gentleman's mastery of writing, record keeping, and other manly skills. Often these portraits were of ministers, schoolteachers, men of commerce, or others of similar stature in the community. Artist R. B. Crafft's solemn portrait of *The Merchant* (below), painted in 1836, is but one example. Note the swags and tassels in the upper left-hand corner of the painting!

FOLLOWING THE DICTATES OF TRADITION, I STITCHED A SECOND version of my pen-in-hand design, right. The original version boasted a

decidedly feminine cuff, so I made this one quintessentially masculine (the cuff, I fancied, of a sea captain or a soldier). I kept the background sober (a sort of banker's pinstripe) and the border subdued. Framed, the picture makes a splendid gift, I think, for any man who spends his days signing letters or correcting papers, or for one who secretly aspires to penning the Great American Novel.

AS WITH MANY OF THE DESIGNS IN THIS BOOK, ELEMENTS OF MY QUILL PEN POR-TRAITS CAN BE SELECTED OUT FOR SMALLER PROJECTS. ABOVE, I CREATED A SIMPLE INKWELL SHAPE TO HOLD A SIM-PLIFIED VERSION OF THE LADY'S QUILL PEN AND LOOPED A BOW AROUND THE QUILL FOR A TOUCH OF ROMANCE. YOU SHOULD BE ABLE TO STITCH UP THIS SIM-PLE MOTIF IN AN HOUR OR SO. BACK IT WITH FELT TO MAKE A BOOK-MARK, OR TURN IT INTO A FABRIC-LINED CASE FOR READING GLASSES. A BLOCKIER INKWELL AND RIBBON-LESS QUILL WOULD BE A MORE SUITABLE MOTIF FOR A MAN'S MEMENTO.

"WELCOME BABY" WAS THE TRADI-
tional salute to a newborn in days gone by.
Often, the message was carefully spelled
out in steel pins on a satin cushion by an
older child in the family and presented to
mother when the new brother or sister
arrived, as a memento of the occasion. I
find it a charming message for a new
arrival, so I picked up the swag and tassel
corner from my quill design, reshaped the border, and stitched up the
greeting as a baby gift. I'm partial to the cream and gold color scheme at
left, but I also worked up the design in pinks and blues for the tradition-
alists on my baby gift list.

FOR THE LETTERING OF THE MESSAGE, I USED A LOVELY OLD-
fashioned alphabet, which you'll find in charted form in Chapter Six. You
may prefer to substitute a different motto, or add details such as the baby's
name and date of birth. To do this, use the letters and numbers on pages
123–124 to compose your message, center it on canvas of the appropriate
size and shape, then adapt the border design to fit. Graph paper is helpful
in arranging the spacing of letters and words.

IF YOU HAVE NO NEED FOR BABY GIFTS AT THE MOMENT,
stitch whatever you like inside the border: a name, a line of poetry, words of praise or celebration. This is another of several border designs in the book that would work particularly well as a
picture frame. Adjust the coloring of the frame and the shape and
size of the center opening to suit the picture you plan to display.
(Tips for stitching frames are included in Chapter Six.)

THESE PASTEL SHADES ARE FITTING AND PROPER FOR BABY GIFTS, BUT THE FRAME WOULD ALSO BE SMASHING STITCHED IN RICH TONES OF GARNET OR AMBER OR FOREST GREEN, DON'T YOU THINK?

LIKE THE CHEERFUL ENTOMOLOGIST OUT TO SNAG A BUTTERFLY ON THE SCRAP OF REDWORK EMBROIDERY ABOVE, I HUNT FOR DESIGN IDEAS ALL OVER THE LANDSCAPE—AND EVERYTHING IS FAIR GAME FOR MY NEEDLE. I HOPE THE VARIOUS SOURCES I'VE SUGGESTED THROUGHOUT THESE PAGES WILL INSPIRE YOU TO LOOK AT YOUR SURROUNDINGS WITH A FRESH AND EAGER EYE. HAPPILY, INSPIRATION IS EVERYWHERE.

A HEART IN HAND MAY WELL BE THE most familiar of all American folk art designs. The motif most often appears as an open hand with a heart in the center: traditional symbol of generosity, and an accepted token of affection freely offered or gratefully received. But, as usual, I needed to put my own twist on tradition. I wanted my heart-in-hand design to be a little less sentimental and a lot more festive. I wanted it to be bright and sassy and slightly silly—a jolly needlepoint valentine. And that's exactly how it turned out!

SOMETIMES IT'S DIFFICULT TO FIGURE OUT EXACTLY WHERE THE different elements of a pattern come from, but somehow they all filter through an individual sensibility and combine to form a uniquely personal design. I love the tiny little heart held in a large and trusting hand, the contrast between the darkly patterned background and the zingy border, and the way the scalloped heart frills seem to dance in waves around the edges of this design. The red-on-white pattern reminds me of the cheerful eyelet curtains with red piping and embroidered patterns that fluttered in the kitchen windows of cottages by the sea where I spent my summers as a child. The whole design is a total happiness to me.

A SINGLE FLOUNCE OF THE HEART BORDER STITCHED AROUND A small initialed square is perfect for the little makeup case at left. Adapt a similar design to stitch on a wee pincushion or other personal gifts.

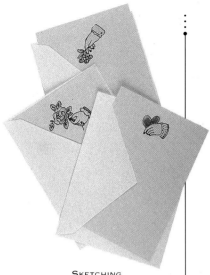

$\mathcal{A}$s YOU MAY HAVE GATHERED FROM THE WEALTH OF SOURCE materials mentioned throughout this book, I'm an avid fan of collecting and recycling motifs, patterns, and design ideas. I believe in saving everything—even my own discarded sketches and color studies—for possible use another day.

$\mathcal{M}$ANY OF US ARE TIMID WHEN IT COMES TO DRAWING, AND ARE therefore convinced that we'll never be able to create our own needlepoint designs. But here's where practice leads to confidence, if not necessarily to perfection. I practice my sketching all the time—trying not to copy things exactly, but to capture the spirit of a gesture, the shape of an object, the scale and relationship of elements in a design. Even though many of my drawings never find their way into finished needlepoint pictures, I find that the simplest stream-of-consciousness, off-the-cuff doodle often has a spontaneity and a quirky personal quality it would be a shame to waste.

$\mathcal{P}$ICTURED HERE ARE SAMPLE PEN AND INK SKETCHES THAT I made while working on designs for *A Show of Hands*. I snipped out a few of my favorites and took the clippings down to my local print shop to be reproduced on cream cardstock in black and white. I hand-tinted each printed card with a dash of watercolor or colored pencil, and sent one off from time to time over the last two years to reassure myself and friends that there was indeed a "work in progress." Now that this book is done, the cards are happy mementos of the creative process that brought it to fruition, and a reminder that no step in the evolution of a design need ever go to waste.

SKETCHING AND RESKETCHING MOTIFS IS ONE OF THE WAYS I MANAGE TO CALM MY OWN TREPIDATIONS AS A DESIGNER. OFTEN I FIND THAT MY QUICK SKETCHES HAVE A SPONTANEOUS QUALITY THAT IT TAKES HOURS TO RECAPTURE IN NEEDLEPOINT. TO PARAPHRASE A POPULAR MAXIM, "THERE'S MANY A SLIP 'TWIXT SKETCH AND STITCH."

THE PATTERNS

◆ 18 x 18-INCH SQUARE OF NO. 12 MONO CANVAS.

◆ NO. 20 TAPESTRY NEEDLE.

◆ 3-STRAND PATERNAYAN PERSIAN WOOL OR OTHER NEEDLEPOINT YARN IN THE FOLLOWING COLORS AND APPROXIMATE AMOUNTS:

No.	Color	Yds.
202	Steel Gray	35
204	Lt. Steel Gray	8
321	Plum	4
462	Med. Beige Brown	22
463	Lt. Beige Brown	6
491	Med. Flesh	3
493	Lt. Flesh	6
496	Med. Wicker Brown	4
504	Federal Blue	52
555	Ice Blue	130
583	Dk. Sky Blue	2
584	Med. Sky Blue	4
703	Lt. Butterscotch	5
753	Med. Old Gold	18
755	Lt. Old Gold	13
860	Dk. Copper	4
863	Med. Copper	4
910	Dk. Dusty Pink	1
912	Med. Dusty Pink	5

LADY'S QUILL PEN

$\mathcal{T}$O CREATE THE 14 x 14-INCH DESIGN PICTURED ON PAGE 86, PREPARE an 18 x 18-inch piece of number 12 mono canvas following instructions in Chapter Six. Bind the edges of the canvas with masking tape and sketch in the design with permanent needlepoint markers to match yarn colors. Use two strands of yarn to stitch the design.

$\mathcal{R}$EFERRING TO THE CHARTED PATTERN AND ACCOMPANYING color code, first outline the cuff and hand in continental stitch, work the polka dots and pleats, then fill in the cuff and hand in basketweave. Next, outline and stitch the feathered quill pen.

$\mathcal{S}$TITCH THE INNER BORDER, THEN FILL IN THE BACKGROUND square and initial block. Finally, plot and stitch the border. General instructions for completing the cardcase pictured on page 87 and the petit point letterbox insert shown on page 88 are given in Chapter Six.

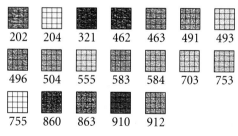

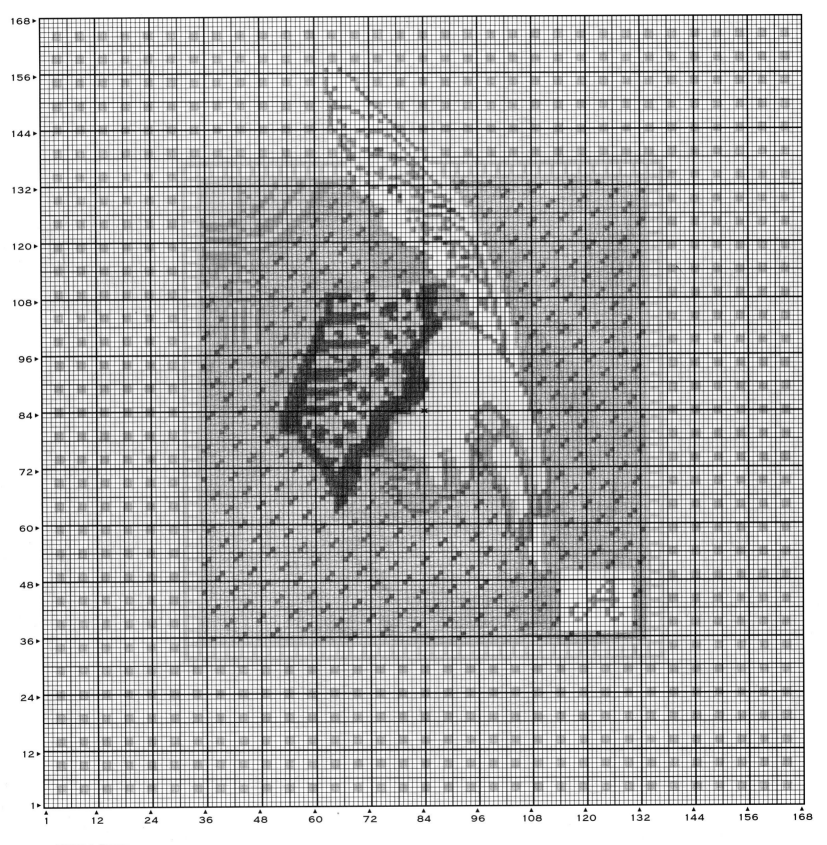

WHAT YOU'LL NEED

◆ 18 x 18-INCH SQUARE OF NO. 12 MONO CANVAS.

◆ NO. 20 TAPESTRY NEEDLE.

◆ 3-STRAND PATERNAYAN PERSIAN WOOL OR OTHER NEEDLEPOINT YARN IN THE FOLLOWING COLORS AND APPROXIMATE AMOUNTS:

No.	Color	Yds.
204	Steel Gray	5
220	Black	2
262	Cream	7
451	Dk. Khaki Brown	23
452	Med. Khaki Brown	50
453	Med. Lt. Khaki Brown	6
454	Lt. Khaki Brown	3
490	Med. Flesh	3
493	Lt. Flesh	4
500	Dk. Federal Blue	10
501	Dk. Med. Federal Blue	2
502	Med. Federal Blue	2
504	Lt. Federal Blue	2
581	Sky Blue	11
732	Lt. Honey Gold	3
733	Med. Honey Gold	3
863	Copper	4
880	Ginger	2
922	Med. Wood Rose	60
923	Lt. Wood Rose	125

GENTLEMAN'S QUILL PEN

*T*O CREATE THE 14 x 14-INCH DESIGN PICTURED ON PAGE 91, PREPARE an 18x18-inch piece of number 12 mono canvas following instructions in Chapter Six. Bind the edges of the canvas with masking tape and sketch in the design with permanent needlepoint markers to match yarn colors. Use two strands of yarn to stitch the design.

*R*EFERRING TO THE CHARTED PATTERN AND ACCOMPANYING color code, first outline the cuff and hand in continental stitch, then fill in the motifs in basketweave. Next, outline and stitch the feathered quill pen.

*S*TITCH THE INNER BORDER, THEN FILL IN THE BACKGROUND square and initial block. Finally, plot and stitch the border. General instructions for framing completed needlepoint pieces are given in Chapter Six.

204	220	262	451	452	453	454

490	493	500	501	502	504	581

732	733	863	880	922	923

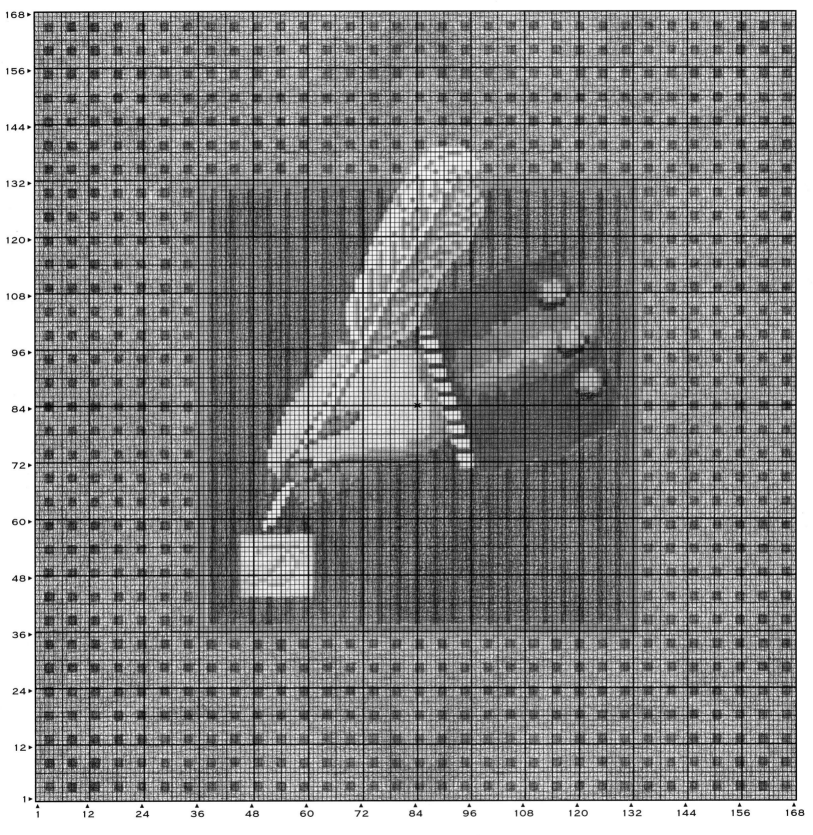

✕ MIDDLE POINT

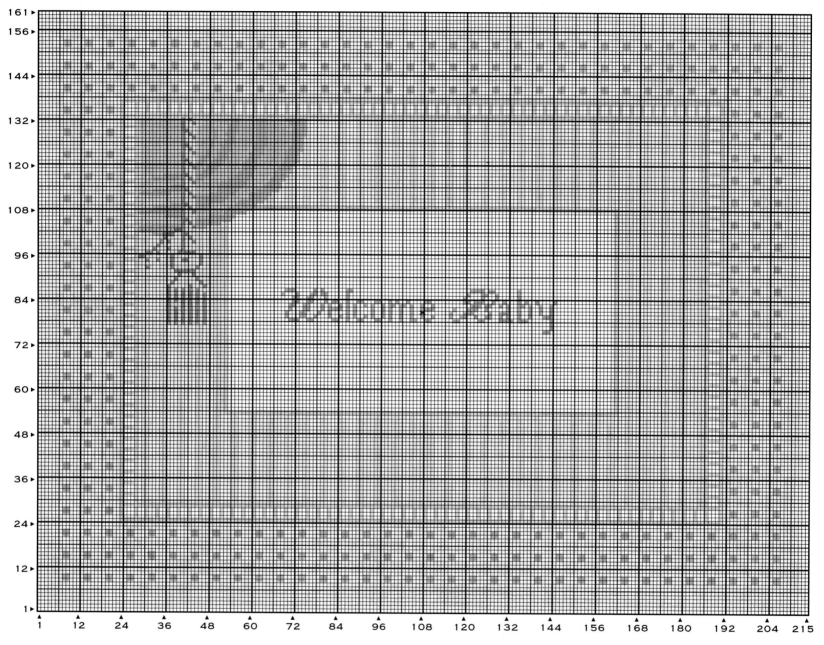

x Middle Point

WELCOME BABY

$\mathcal{T}$O CREATE THE 7 1/4 X 9 3/8-INCH PETIT POINT DESIGN PICTURED on page 92, prepare a 9 1/2 x 11 1/2-inch piece of number 18 mono canvas following instructions in Chapter Six. Bind the edges of the canvas with masking tape and sketch in the outlines of the design with permanent needlepoint markers to match yarn colors. I use single strands of yarn to stitch the design.

$\mathcal{T}$HE CHARTED PATTERN AND INSTRUCTIONS ARE TO COMPLETE the blue and white Welcome Baby design. To create either the gold and white or pink and white design, retain white and gold for the inner rectangle, inner border, and tassel, and substitute colors of your choice for the striped background, curtain swag, and polka-dot frame.

$\mathcal{F}$IRST, PLOT AND STITCH THE MOTTO IN THE CENTER OF THE design, using continental stitch. Work the background of the motto in white basketweave stitch and frame with a single row of Medium Old Gold. Sketch and stitch the second border of gold and white squares, then fill in the corner swag, tassel, and striped background. Finally, complete the polka-dot border. Frame as desired, following the tips in Chapter Six.

WHAT YOU'LL NEED

◆ 9 1/2 x 11 1/2-INCH PIECE OF NO. 18 MONO CANVAS.

◆ No. 22 TAPESTRY NEEDLE.

◆ 3-STRAND PATERNAYAN PERSIAN WOOL OR OTHER NEEDLEPOINT YARN IN THE FOLLOWING COLORS AND APPROXIMATE AMOUNTS:

No.	COLOR	YDS.
260	White	50
496	Med. Wicker Brown	6
504	Federal Blue	40
507	Lightest Federal Blue	65
555	Ice Blue	100
583	Dk. Sky Blue	8
584	Med. Sky Blue	10
703	Lt. Butterscotch	8
732	Med. Honey Gold	7
753	Med. Old Gold	30

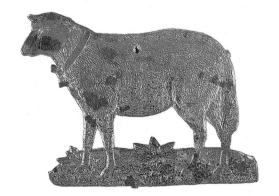

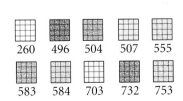

260 496 504 507 555

583 584 703 732 753

WHAT YOU'LL NEED

◆ 18 x 18-INCH SQUARE OF NO. 12 MONO CANVAS.

◆ NO. 20 TAPESTRY NEEDLE.

◆ 3-STRAND PATERNAYAN PERSIAN WOOL OR OTHER NEEDLEPOINT YARN IN THE FOLLOWING COLORS AND APPROXIMATE AMOUNTS:

No.	Color	Yds.
260	*White*	55
262	*Cream*	3
493	*Lt. Flesh*	4
500	*Dk. Federal Blue*	38
551	*Dk. Ice Blue*	50
552	*Med. Ice Blue*	30
590	*Med. Flesh*	5
593	*Caribbean Blue*	7
696	*Christmas Red*	1
863	*Copper*	4
902	*Darkest American Beauty*	60
903	*Dk. American Beauty*	40
904	*Med. American Beauty*	56
905	*Med. Lt. American Beauty*	64
906	*Lt. American Beauty*	65
907	*Lightest American Beauty*	48

VALENTINE

*T*O CREATE THE 14 x 14-INCH DESIGN PICTURED ON PAGE 95, PREPARE an 18 x 18-inch piece of number 12 mono canvas following instructions in Chapter Six. Bind the edges of the canvas with masking tape and sketch in the design with permanent needlepoint markers to match yarn colors. Use two strands of yarn to stitch the design.

*R*EFERRING TO THE CHARTED PATTERN AND ACCOMPANYING color code, first outline the hand and cuff in continental stitch, then complete the motifs in basketweave. Stitch in the tiny valentine card.

*P*LOT AND STITCH THE INNER BORDER, THEN FILL IN THE background. Finally, work the border scallops, row by row, and fill in the remaining background of the border. Hints on stitching the little makeup case pictured on page 94 appear in Chapter Six.

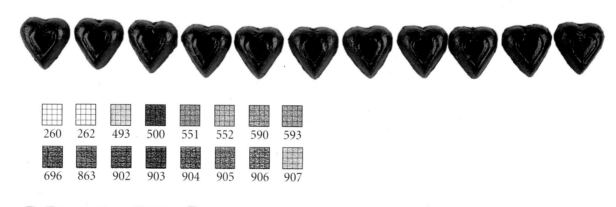

260	262	493	500	551	552	590	593

696	863	902	903	904	905	906	907

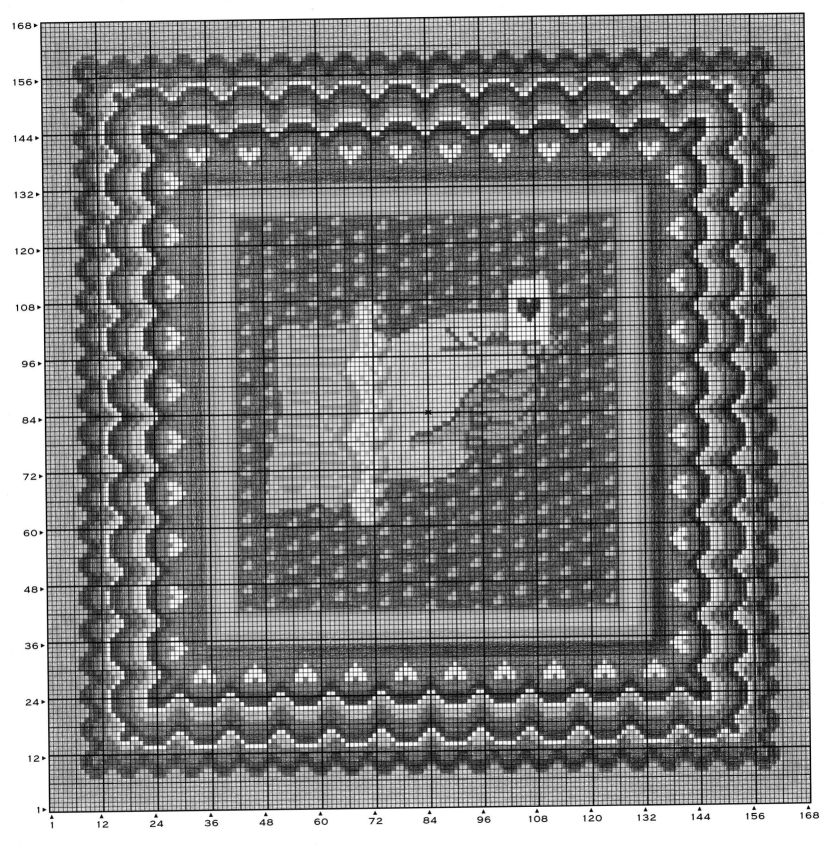

168▶
156▶
144▶
132▶
120▶
108▶
96▶
84▶
72▶
60▶
48▶
36▶
24▶
12▶
1▶

1   12   24   36   48   60   72   84   96   108   120   132   144   156   168

✕ Middle Point

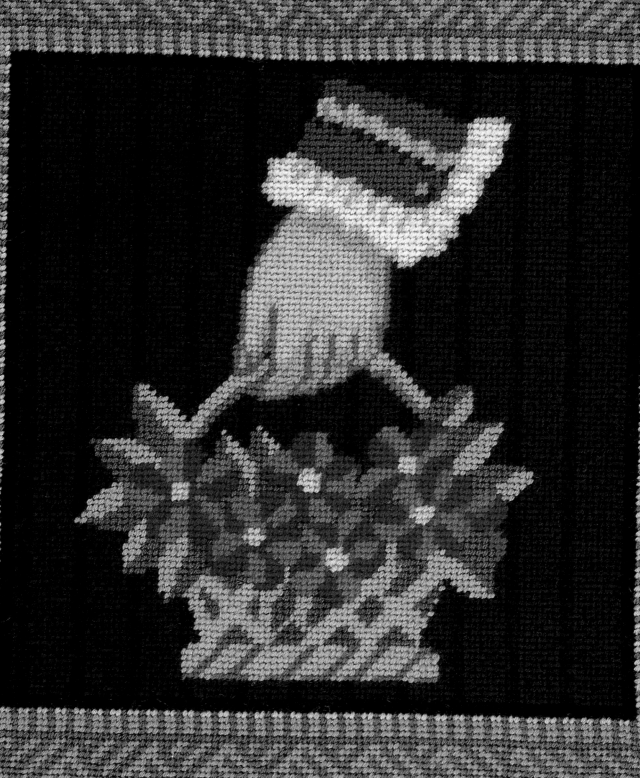

Chapter Six

NEEDLEPOINT BASICS

THE BASIC INS AND OUTS OF NEEDLE-POINT ARE RELATIVELY EASY TO MASTER, BUT TRANSLATING DESIGNS INTO FINISHED STITCHERY OFTEN TAKES A BIT OF DOING. THIS CHAPTER PROVIDES INSTRUCTIONS ON HOW TO STITCH AND FINISH THE PROJECTS IN THIS BOOK PLUS TIPS ON ADAPTING THESE PATTERNS TO CREATE DESIGNS OF YOUR OWN.

THE TRIO OF FLOWER BASKET DESIGNS ABOVE ALL CONTRIBUTED TO THE FINAL NEEDLEPOINT DESIGN PICTURED ON PAGE 106. AS YOU CAN SEE, THE POSSIBLE VARIATIONS ON SHAPES, COLORS, AND STYLE FOR SUCH A DESIGN ARE ENDLESS.

As I've suggested elsewhere in *A Show of Hands*, sources of inspiration for needlepoint design are everywhere available to us in our daily lives. I believe in using the simplest techniques and the best available materials to translate those designs into finished stitcheries.

Here and on the following pages, you'll find basic information on how to transfer charted patterns onto canvas, a description of the materials and the two simple stitches used to create this collection of designs, plus suggestions on how to finish and mount completed stitcheries. These instructions presume a basic familiarity with the vocabulary and techniques of needlepoint. If you require more detailed information on stitching or finishing techniques, please consult one of the many excellent needlepoint manuals available at your local library or bookstore, or seek advice from experts at the nearest needlework shop.

MATERIALS

For each of these designs I used Zweigart's Wichelt Deluxe Mono Canvas (number 12 for the major designs and number 18 for the petit point variations) and 3-ply Paternayan Persian Wool. The Wichelt canvas is marvelously supple and holds its shape well, while the Paternayan yarns have an excellent feel and come in a range of hues I find particularly well suited to my personal color sense. Feel free to substitute whatever canvas or yarns are available in your local needlepoint shop.

Yarn estimates accompanying each pattern are generous. You may have yarn left over after completing a given project, but I wanted to be sure that you would always have enough yarn of each color to cover any ripping out or restitching that needs to be done. Use leftover strands for practice stitching and to work up smaller projects or sample border patterns for your "files."

Whether you are working on regular or petit point canvas, I suggest you stitch with strands of yarn approximately 16 to 18 inches long. Any longer and the yarn tends to fray and tangle as you stitch.

Always use a blunt tapestry needle of a size to match the canvas gauge for stitching (number 20 for most projects; number 22 for petit point designs). Sharp pointed needles will split the canvas and the yarn and cause no end of snagging and tangling.

PREPARING CANVAS

Cut canvas at least 2 inches larger on all sides than the finished size of the design (i.e., for a 14x14-inch design, use an 18x18-inch square of canvas). Bind the edges of the canvas with masking tape to prevent raveling.

TRANSFERRING CHARTED DESIGNS TO CANVAS

Use waterproof needlepoint markers (or thinned acryllic paints) to transfer designs from chart to canvas.

First, and most importantly, locate and lightly mark the center horizontal and vertical threads of the canvas (I use a pale gray waterproof marker). Center points are indicated on each charted pattern, and marking the corresponding vertical and horizontal axis threads on the canvas will aid you in counting out and plotting the design.

When working with a charted design, remember that each colored square on the chart represents one stitch, taken over a pair of crossed threads on the canvas.

Many stitchers prefer to work directly from charted design to canvas, but if you prefer to transfer the design to the canvas before beginning to stitch, carefully sketch in the general outlines of the design. Keep in mind that you may have to alter the outline by a stitch or two to the right or left, up or down, as the design evolves on the canvas.

I find it useful to color in large areas of the canvas—particularly those to be stitched in dark colors—with needlepoint markers matching the yarn color. This step prevents any white canvas threads showing through on the finished stitchery.

NEEDLEPOINT FRAMES

Many needlepoint experts insist that you use a wooden frame to mount and stitch designs, but I've always found it more satisfying to work without a frame, so that I can roll up my work-in-progress, stash it in my bag, and haul it out to stitch a row or two whenever time permits. A frame does help to keep the stitchery square and makes blocking easier in the end (particularly if you are a tense stitcher and tend to pull each stitch very tight). But if you use the basketweave stitch to fill in large areas of color, as I do, and if the tension of your stitches is generally smooth and even, both will help to keep the canvas square, even if it is hand-held.

A useful alternative to the traditional, rigid needlepoint frame is a portable snap-together frame originally designed for quilting and available in many needlework shops. It can be disassembled easily and stashed in your work bay, then pulled out and reassembled for stitching sessions.

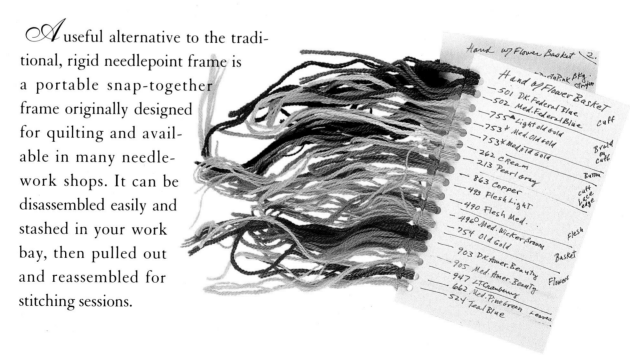

BASIC NEEDLEPOINT STITCHES

*A*ll the designs in this book are worked in a combination of two simple stitches: continental stitch (also known as tent or outline stitch) and basketweave stitch. Both stitches are diagrammed below, but novice needlepointers may want to consult a stitchery textbook for more extensive how-to information.

◆ CONTINENTAL STITCH: Use continental stitch to outline designs and fill in small areas of color. Avoid using this stitch for larger areas because it tends to distort the canvas. Work rows of stitches horizontally from right to left, and reverse the canvas (turning it 180 degrees) to stitch alternate rows.

To stitch, refer to Diagram, below. Bring the needle up at #1, thrust down at #2, and bring up again at #3, etc. Stitches should always slant in the same direction, from lower left to upper right.

◆ BASKETWEAVE STITCH: Use basketweave to fill in large areas of pattern and to work backgrounds. Rows of stitches are worked alternately up and down along the diagonal. To stitch, refer to Diagram, below. Bring the needle up at #1, down at #2, and up again at #3, etc. Stitches should always slant in the same direction, from lower left to upper right.

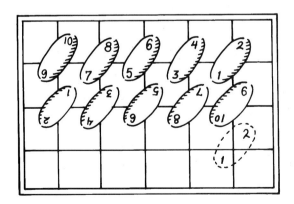

CONTINENTAL STITCH

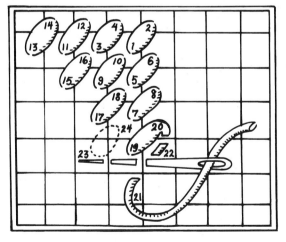

BASKETWEAVE STITCH

A NOTE ON STITCHING AND RIPPING

I OFTEN FIND IT NECESSARY TO STITCH IN AND RIP OUT SMALL AREAS OF COLOR WHEN I'M DEVELOPING A DESIGN.

A SINGLE LINE OR TWO OF CONTINENTAL OR BASKETWEAVE STITCH CAN BE REMOVED BY UNTHREADING THE NEEDLE AND USING ITS POINT TO PULL OUT THE STITCHES ONE BY ONE. BUT DON'T DO THIS MORE THAN ONCE OR TWICE WITH A SINGLE STRAND OF YARN, BECAUSE THE WOOL WILL BEGIN TO FRAY. TO RIP OUT LARGER AREAS, USE A PAIR OF SMALL, SHARP SCISSORS TO SNIP OUT THE OFFENDING STITCHES, PRESERVING A TAIL ABOUT 4 INCHES LONG TO BE WOVEN INTO THE BACK OF THE REMAINING STITCHED SECTION. SNIP THROUGH EACH STITCH INDIVIDUALLY, TAKING CARE NOT TO CUT THE UNDERLYING CANVAS. PULL AWAY ALL THE CLIPPED THREADS BEFORE BEGINNING AGAIN WITH FRESH YARN.

WHAT YOU'LL NEED

◆ 18 x 18-INCH SQUARE OF NO. 12 MONO CANVAS.

◆ No. 20 TAPESTRY NEEDLE.

◆ 3-STRAND PATERNAYAN PERSIAN WOOL OR OTHER NEEDLEPOINT YARN IN THE FOLLOWING COLORS AND APPROXIMATE AMOUNTS:

No.	Color	Yds.
213	Pearl Gray	3
262	Cream	4
310	Grape	15
442	Med. Golden Brown	11
490	Med. Flesh	3
493	Lt. Flesh	4
496	Med. Wicker Brown	110
501	Dk. Federal Blue	2
502	Med. Federal Blue	4
524	Teal Blue	7
570	Navy Blue	12
662	Pine Green	7
734	Honey Gold	100
753	Dk. Old Gold	3
754	Med. Old Gold	5
755	Lt. Old Gold	9
863	Copper	3
903	Dk. American Beauty	7
905	Med. American Beauty	7
910	Dusty Pink	75
947	Lt. Cranberry	4

To CREATE THE 14 x 14-INCH DESIGN PICTURED ON PAGE 106, PREPARE an 18 x 18-inch piece of number 12 mono canvas following instructions in Chapter Six. Bind the edges of the canvas with masking tape and sketch in the design with permanent needlepoint markers to match yarn colors. Use two strands of yarn to stitch the design.

*R*EFERRING TO THE CHARTED PATTERN AND ACCOMPANYING color code, first outline the hand and cuff in continental stitch, then complete these motifs in basketweave. Next, outline and fill in the basket, posies, and leaves.

*T*HEN, PLOT AND STITCH THE INNER BORDER AND COMPLETE the striped background for the center square in basketweave stitch.

*B*EFORE BEGINNING TO WORK THE LATTICE BORDER, STITCH diagonal lines of Light Old Gold from each corner of the inner border to the corresponding outer corners of the canvas. Following the chart, stitch the Basketry border from the top right-hand corner of the design to the top left-hand corner, turn and stitch the next border, and so on. It should all fall easily into place. Instructions for completing the petit point Basketry picture frame shown on page 115 appear on the following pages.

213	262	310	442	490	493	496	501	502

524	570	662	734	753	754	755	863	903

905	910	947

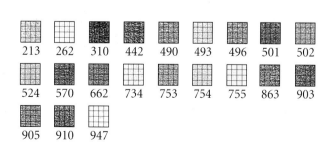

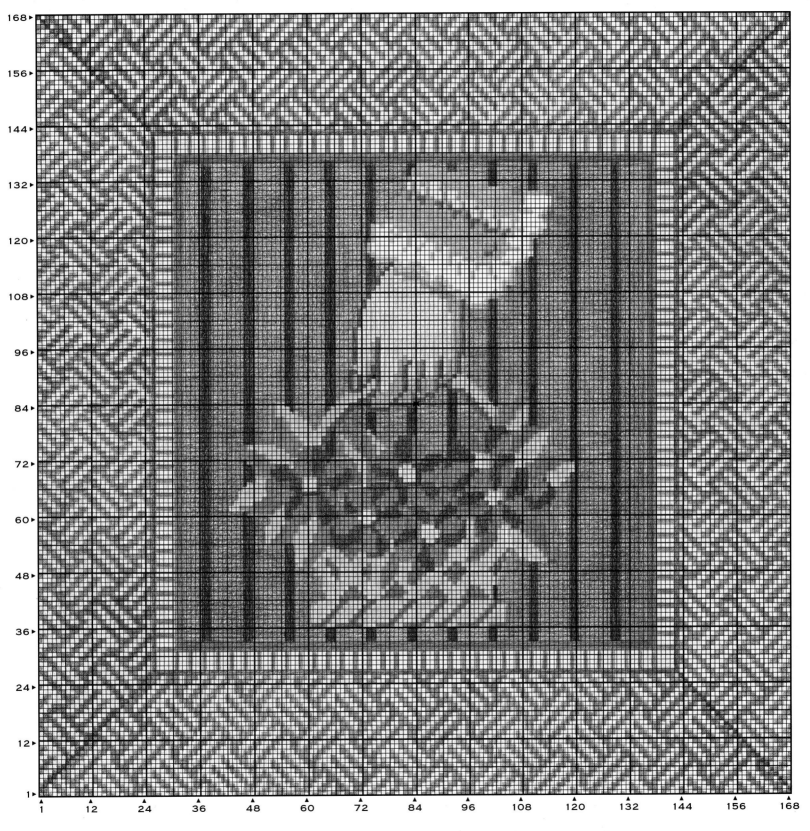

X MIDDLE POINT

WHAT YOU'LL NEED

◆ 12 x 12-INCH SQUARE
OF NO. 18 MONO CANVAS.

◆ NO. 22 TAPESTRY NEEDLE.

◆ DMC COTTON EMBROI-
DERY FLOSS IN THE FOL-
LOWING COLORS AND
APPROXIMATE AMOUNTS:

No.	Color	Yds.
436	Med. Wicker Brown	40
676	Honey Gold	40
3045	Med. Golden Brown	8
3047	Lt. Old Gold	5

THE SMALL NEEDLEPOINT PURSE (RIGHT), STITCHED IN COTTON FLOSS AROUND THE TURN OF THE CENTURY, IS EMBLAZONED WITH THE KIND OF FREE-FORM, IMPRESSIONISTIC POSIES I LOVE. THE COLORS ON THIS PURSE HAVE FADED OVER THE YEARS, BUT THE ARTLESSLY STITCHED PETALS AND UNEXPECTED HUES INSPIRED THE MIX OF SHAPES AND COLORS ON MY FLOWER BASKET DESIGN (PAGE 106).

TIPS ON PETIT POINT

*T*hough most of the designs in this collection are worked on number 12 mono canvas, any and all of the designs can be worked on larger or smaller gauge canvas, to yield a finished stitchery of a size to suit your needs.

To create dainty petit point designs (such as the Flower Basket guest book cover on page 107 or the Basketry picture frame at right—both adapted from the Flower Basket pattern on page 106), transfer any given pattern to number 18 mono canvas and stitch the design using a single strand of Persian Wool or 6 strands of DMC Cotton Embroidery Floss and a number 22 tapestry needle.

In general, guesstimate that the amount of yarn needed to stitch a design on petit point (number 18) canvas will be approximately two thirds of the yardage required to stitch the same design on the larger gauged number 12 canvas. Yarn colors, of course, will remain the same.

Cotton floss has a wonderful, silky sheen and is an interesting alternative to wool yarn for petit point designs that will not receive extended wear. To stitch a petit point design in cotton floss, as I have done for the Basketry frame pictured here, choose skeins of DMC Cotton Floss in colors that approximate those of the original yarn pattern. (As an example, cotton floss yardage requirements to stitch this Basketry picture frame are given in the column at left).

To complete the frame, see instructions on page 117.

BLOCKING

*M*ost pieces of needlepoint, even those stitched on a frame, will need to be blocked before mounting. Professional blocking services are available through many needlepoint and fabric shops, but blocking can also be done at home.

First, lightly steam-press the needlepoint on the wrong side to soften the canvas and even out the stitches, and to give yourself an idea of how much blocking you'll have to do.

Next, you'll need a clean board (l/4- or l/2-inch plywood works well), a piece of sheeting or a dish towel, a straight edge (such as a metal ruler), rustproof thumbtacks, and a hammer.

Cover board with fabric and staple or thumbtack in place. Then, using the straight edge, measure and mark a square on the fabric-covered board that is the exact size of the finished design. Use light pencil strokes to outline the square and make sure that the corners of the square are perfect right angles. Thumbtack the stitchery facedown on the board, working from the center of each side out toward corners, carefully matching the corners of the stitchery with the sketched corners on the fabric-covered board.

The canvas and yarn are both strong and pliant, so don't be afraid to pull and tug your stitchery into a squared shape. Once the piece is in place, dampen the back of the needlepoint with a mister or sponge. Allow the needlepoint to dry completely. It may be necessary to repeat this process until you achieve the desired effect. When the needlepoint is properly squared and completely dry, remove from the board and trim the excess canvas to within 3/4 inch of the stitching. Once again, press the piece lightly on the wrong side before mounting or making into a pillow or other project.

TO FRAME NEEDLEPOINT DESIGNS

*T*o frame a blocked needlepoint picture, cut a piece of cardboard or foamcore l/8-inch smaller than the finished size of the stitchery. Stretch the

FOR ME, PART OF THE DELIGHT OF NEEDLEPOINT HAS ALWAYS BEEN THE WONDERFULLY IMAGINATIVE TOOLS, NOTIONS, AND ACCESSORIES THAT ENHANCE THE NEEDLE ARTS. PICTURED HERE ARE TWO OF MY FAVORITES, BOTH DATING FROM THE NINETEENTH CENTURY: A SATIN PINCUSHION IN THE SHAPE OF A PEAPOD AND A SILVER-TOPPED FABRIC STRAWBERRY FILLED WITH EMERY POWDER (USED TO SHARPEN PRECIOUS PINS AND NEEDLES).

needlepoint in place and tack the raw edges to the back of the cardboard or foamcore with masking tape or strong glue. (Alternatively, cover the cardboard with muslin and tack the raw canvas edges to the muslin with needle and thread.) Slip the mounted needlepoint into a ready-made or custom-designed frame.

NEEDLEPOINT PICTURE MATS

To make a needlepoint mat for a picture frame (like the petit point Basketry design pictured on page 115), outline and stitch one of the needlepoint border designs from the patterns in this book, leaving the center square of the design empty. Block and press the piece as described above.

Trim the outer edges of the raw canvas to within 3/4 inch of the stitched pattern. Carefully cut out the inside square of the unstitched canvas to within 1/2 inch of the stitched pattern. Clip the corners of the inner square up to the stitched inner border; turn and press the raw canvas to the wrong side of the design. Press under the outer edges of the canvas, carefully mitering the corners.

Cut a cardboard frame very slightly smaller (1/16 inch on all sides) than the finished needlepoint design. Center the needlepoint mat on top of the cardboard mat and glue in place. Mount the picture or memento in place and settle the framed piece in a purchased or custom-made frame.

NEEDLEPOINT PILLOWS

Choose the backing fabric for your pillow with care. It should be sturdy, but not too heavy to stitch; cotton velveteen or a closely woven, upholstery-weight cotton in a color to match or complement the background of your design is a good choice. If you plan to use fabric-covered cording to trim the pillow, cut, pin, and stitch the cording around the edges of the needlepointed piece (cording should be placed pointing in toward the center of the piece, with cording seam allowance laid over the unstitched canvas seam allowance).

A NOTE ON PILLOWS

SINCE AN AMPLY STUFFED PILLOW HAS A DECIDED CURVE, AND THE EDGE OF THE BORDER PATTERN MAY BE HIDDEN BY THE CURVE OR OBSCURED BY CORDING, YOU MAY WANT TO STITCH AN EXTRA FOUR OR FIVE ROWS OF BORDER AROUND YOUR DESIGN TO MAKE SURE IT IS FULLY VISIBLE WHEN THE PILLOW IS COMPLETED.

A Note on Cording

Most of the cording or trim used to finish projects in this book is ready-made material, widely available in local fabric and upholstery shops. But I also collect odd lengths of antique trim at flea markets and antiques shops, and often use these one-of-a-kind pieces to embellish a special project (see Squirrel Pincushion, p. 33).

To insert a zipper in the backing fabric, cut two pieces of fabric measuring the width by half the height of the finished design; add a 3/4-inch seam allowance on all sides. Piece the two halves of the backing together and stitch the zipper in place along the center seam. Lay the backing on the pillow top, right sides together. Stitch around all four sides, trim the seams, turn, and stuff with a purchased pillow form. I prefer to use down-stuffed forms, but polyester, dacron, or foam pillows are less expensive and more readily available from local needlepoint shops.

If you do not plan to insert a zipper in your finished pillow, simply pin a matching size square of backing fabric to the needlepoint pillow front, right sides together, stitch around three sides of the pillow, trim the seams, turn, stuff, and slip-stitch the fourth side closed. This is the easiest finishing choice, particularly for small pillows and pincushion-size projects.

To edge a pillow with braid or trim other than fabric-covered cording, slip-stitch the trim around the edges of the completed pillow cover, tucking the raw ends of the trim into the seamline of the fourth side of the pillow.

SPECIAL PROJECTS

Following are tips on completing some of the projects in this book that are neither pillows nor framed pictures—projects that have not been covered in the individual pattern instructions or in the basic finishing instructions on the preceding pages.

◆ ROSE WREATH WEDDING ALBUM: The album pictured on page 20 was crafted by a professional bookbinder. To create a similar album, first stitch and block the 7 3/4 x 7 3/4-inch petit point wreath as an inset for the album cover, as described on page 30. Next, mount the petit point design in a fabric-covered mat, cut to size to fit the cover of a purchased photo album (this one measures 14 inches square). Line the inside front cover of the album with matching fabric; bring the raw edges to the front of the cover and glue in place. Cover the back and spine of the album with fabric. Glue the framed petitpoint design to the front cover of the album, concealing all raw edges.

◆ ROSE WREATH RING PILLOW: To make the 8x8-inch ring pillow, complete the petit point wreath design; block and back the stitchery with matching fabric. Stitch the pillow around three sides, turn, stuff, and slip-stitch the fourth side closed. Slip-stitch narrow gold cording around the edges of the pillow, tucking the raw edges of the cording into the seam of the fourth side.

◆ SQUIRREL PINCUSHION: Complete the 7 1/2 x 7 1/2-inch squirrel medallion design on number 12 mono canvas. Block the stitchery, back with matching fabric, stitch, turn, press, and stuff. Stitch novelty or antique trim around the edges of the pincushion; slip the raw ends of the cording into the bottom edge of the pillow and slip-stitch the pillow closed.

◆ SQUIRREL STOOL: Select a purchased wooden footstool kit (see Sources and Suppliers, page 125). Cut a piece of number 12 mono canvas to fit the top of the stool (adding 3/4-inch seam allowance to the edges of the canvas). Center and stitch the squirrel design. Stitch a border to size. Block the completed canvas and mount on the stool top, following kit instructions (center the needlepoint on the stool insert, tack the raw edges of the canvas to the back of the insert, and replace the insert in the stool frame).

◆ DOLL PURSE: To make the 6 1/2 x 6 1/2-inch purse, prepare a 9 x 9-inch square of number 12 mono canvas. Center and stitch the doll design, as described on page 78, angling the lower corners as shown in the photo. Cut three pieces of backing/lining fabric to size (I chose a moiré taffeta); add a 1/2-inch seam allowance all around each piece. With right sides together, stitch the backing piece along the sides and bottom of the needlepoint design; turn and press. With right sides together, stitch the remaining two pieces together as lining; trim the

seams and slip the lining into the purse. Turn under the upper seam allowance and slip-stitch to the front and back of the purse.

For the trim and strap, braid together 1 yard each of three different colors of satin rattail cording. Stitch braided cording to the edges of the purse and leave the remainder of the braid to serve as a purse strap. Tuck the raw edges of the braided cord into the seam and stitch the seam closed.

◆ ROOSTER SCRAPBOOK : Stitch the rooster design, extending the border to match the size of a purchased photo album (ours measures 14 x 14 inches square). Block the stitchery, turn under the raw edges, and glue to the front of the album. Line the album cover with fabric and slip-stitch the edges of the lining to the edges of the needlepointed cover. Slipcover the back of the album with matching fabric. Stitch or glue purchased cording around the edges of the cover. To complete, stitch or glue a knotted bow of cording to the back edge of the cover.

◆ EYEGLASS CASE : Prepare an 8 1/2 x 9-inch piece of number 12 mono canvas and stitch in a border design of your choice, leaving a 1-inch strip of unstitched canvas on all sides. Block the canvas, press in half (wrong sides together), turn under seam allowances, and stitch around the bottom and sides of the case. Cut and stitch the lining pieces; trim seams. Slip the lining inside the finished needlepoint case, turn under the raw edges of the lining around the top, and slip-stitch the lining to the needlepoint case. The finished size is a 6 1/2 x 3 1/2-inch rectangle.

◆ PATCH POCKET : Stitch a small needlepoint motif of your choice on a scrap of canvas at least 1 inch larger all around than the size of the pocket. Block the stitchery and press the raw edges of the canvas to the wrong side. Slip-stitch the needlepointed motif to the front of the sweater pocket.

◆ MONOGRAMMED CARD CASE: To make this 4 x 4 1/2-inch case, prepare a 6 x 6 1/2-inch piece of number 18 mono canvas. Using the picture on page 87 as a guide, plot and stitch a monogram and border adapted from the Quill Pen design. Back and line the card case as described for the doll purse above. Slip-stitch purchased cording around all four edges of the finished case, adding decorative loops of cording at each corner of the case.

◆ LADY'S LETTERBOX: This 10 1/4 x 10 1/4-inch letterbox was crafted by a professional bookbinder specifically to showcase an 8 x 8-inch petit point stitchery of the Lady's Quill Pen design. To create a similar letterbox, mount the finished petit point square atop any purchased box of sturdy cardboard. Frame the design with a fabric-covered mat, as described for the Rose Wreath wedding album (see page 118); cover the remainder of the box with matching fabric.

◆ MONOGRAMMED MAKEUP CASE: To make this 5 x 5-inch case, prepare a 7-inch square of number 12 mono canvas. Using the picture on page 94 as a guide, center and stitch the canvas with a monogram square and border adapted from the Valentine design. Block and press the finished stitchery. Cut a piece of backing fabric to size. Place the top edges of the backing fabric and stitchery together and stitch a length of zipper in place. Fold the backing fabric against the stitchery, right sides together (be sure to leave the zipper open for turning). Stitch around the sides and bottom of the case. Turn the makeup case right side out and press. Slip-stitch narrow purchased cording in place, if desired. Add a purchased tassel to the zipper closure.

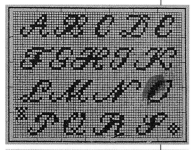

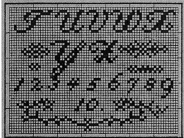

NEEDLEPOINT ALPHABETS

*T*HE PAIR OF ALPHABETS CHARTED ON THESE TWO PAGES WERE adapted from a nineteenth-century pamphlet of alphabets designed for Berlin work (the old name for charted canvas stitchery, so called because the most exquisitely dyed yarns and imaginatively charted patterns came from that German city).

Use either set of letters to compose initial blocks, monograms, or mottoes to personalize any of the designs in this book or other projects of your own creation. The script alphabet, which includes both upper and lower case letters, is best for mottoes (as in the Welcome Baby design on page 92), while the block letters work particularly well for monograms on projects with a more masculine feel (such as the plaid pillow on page 24).

You will find it helpful to use graph paper to center and space letters or messages within a given area. The size and shape of initial blocks on the Lady's Quill Pen (page 86) and Gentleman's Quill Pen (page 91), for example, can be altered to suit the size and shape of the letter(s) you want to use.

As with other designs in the book, use two strands of 3-ply Paternayan Persian Wool to stitch the letters and numbers on number 12 mono canvas, or a single strand to work on number 18 (petit point) canvas. Work the letters first in continental stitch, then fill in the background color in basketweave.

Although I've not used metallic threads on any of these designs, such thread is available in needlepoint shops and would add an appealing touch of elegance to monograms or initials on these and other designs, if you like.

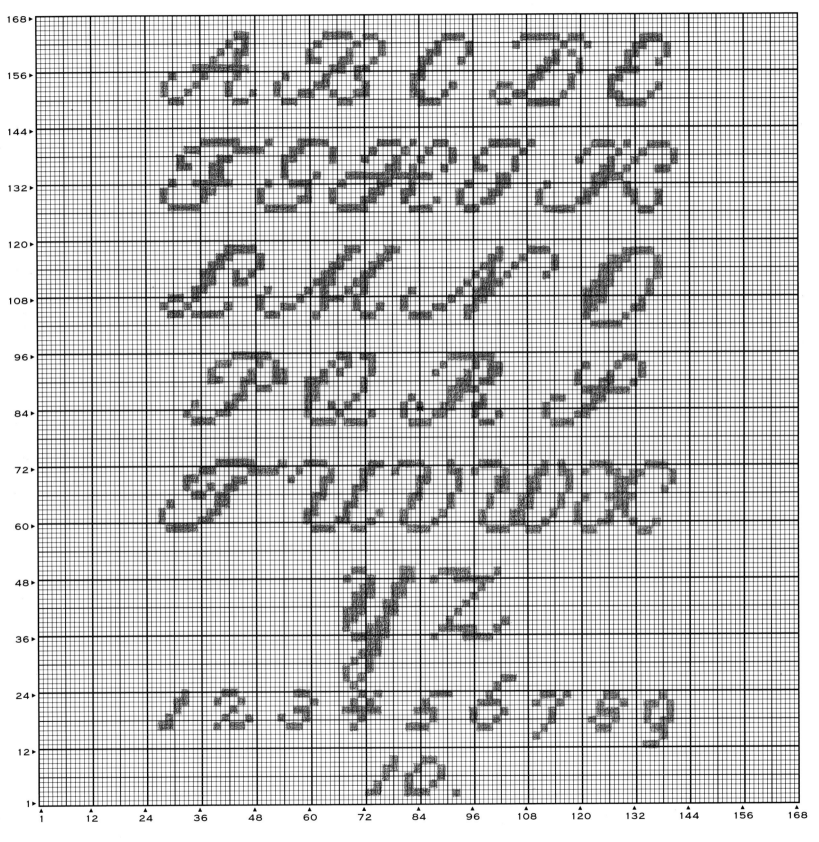

x Middle Point

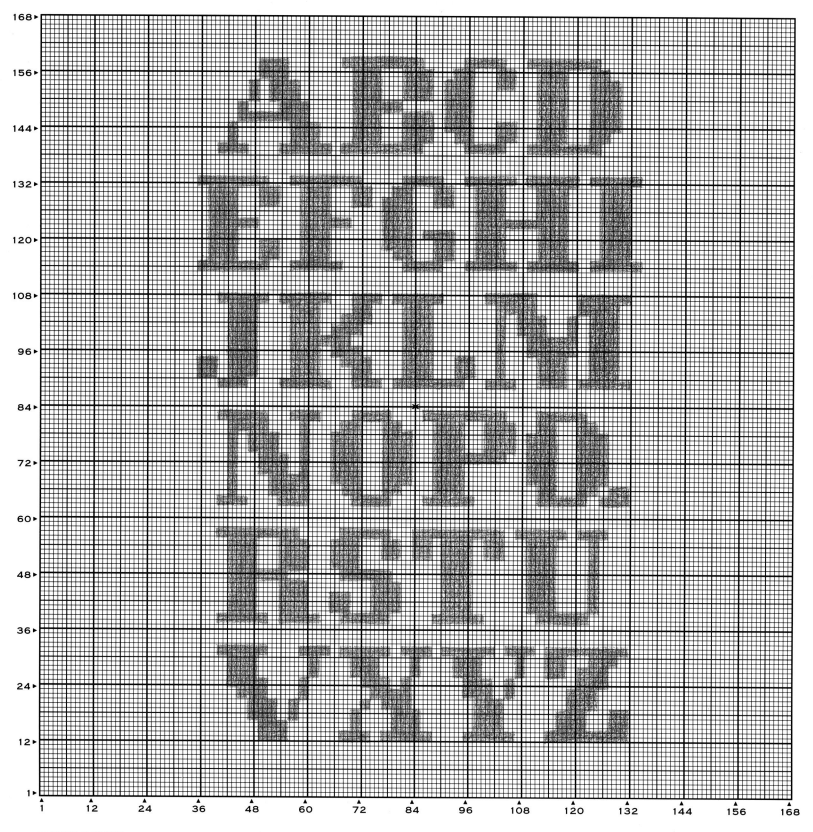

Sources and Suppliers

Photographs

All photographs for *A Show of Hands* are the work of Starr Ockenga, with the following exceptions:

PAGE 11: Photograph of Janet McCaffery by Pieter Estersohn courtesy of *Victoria Magazine*.

PAGE 12: Portrait of *Mother with Three Daughters* courtesy of The Chrysler Museum, Norfolk, VA, gift of Edgar William and Bernice Chrysler Garbisch, 76.53.2b.

PAGE 17: Portrait of Deborah Glen courtesy of The Abby Aldrich Rockefeller Folk Art Center, Williamsburg, VA.

PAGE 34: Portrait of *Boy with Finch* courtesy of The Abby Aldrich Rockefeller Folk Art Center, Williamsburg, VA.

PAGE 55: Portrait of *Girl Holding Cherries* courtesy of The Abby Aldrich Rockefeller Folk Art Center, Williamsburg, VA.

PAGE 90: Portrait of *The Merchant* courtesy of The Abby Aldrich Rockefeller Folk Art Center, Williamsburg, VA.

Props and Support Materials

All furniture and objects photographed in *A Show of Hands* are from the personal collections of artist Janet McCaffery and photographer Starr Ockenga, with the following exceptions:

PAGE 19: Black and white checked shawl, Lyme Regis, Ltd., 68 Thompson Street, New York, N.Y. 10012 (Tel. 212-334-2110).

PAGE 20: Striped wallpaper ("Newport Stripe"), Hines & Co., 979 Third Avenue, New York, N.Y. 10022 (Tel. 212-754-5880); wedding book: This and other handbound books and boxes in *A Show of Hands* were produced by Barbara Mauriello, 231 Garden Street, Hoboken, N.J. 07030 (Tel. 201-420-6613).

PAGE 37: Fabric balls, Susan Parrish, 390 Bleecker Street, New York, N.Y. 10014 (Tel. 212-645-5020); mahogany stool, to be ordered from Freeman & Co., P.O. Box 362, Thomasville, N.C. 27360 (Tel. 919-476-4936).

PAGE 38: Barn door backdrop, c.i.t.e., 100 Wooster Street, New York, N.Y. 10012 (Tel. 212-431-7272).

PAGES 52 AND 53: Striped wallpaper, Clarence House, 211 East 58th Street, New York, N.Y. 10022 (Tel. 212-752-2890); antique table, c.i.t.e. (see above).

PAGE 54: Wallpaper ("Petite Trifle"), Cowan & Tout, 979 Third Avenue, New York, N.Y. 10022 (Tel. 212-753-4488); striped ticking fabric, Cowan & Tout (see above); wide striped fabric, Clarence House (see above); blue hat box, Susan Parrish (see above).

PAGE 57: Red-on-red print wallpaper, Clarence House (see page 125); candlesticks and table, c.i.t.e. (see page 125).

PAGE 73: Early American mechanical tumbler in cloth costume and Early American painted tin goat on platform, Hillman Gallery (Tel. 212-580-1939 or 212-874-0220), by appt. only; red and white ticking and painted toy chest, Susan Parrish (see page 125); red, yellow, and blue striped fabric, Osborne & Little, 979 Third Avenue, New York, N.Y. 10022 (Tel. 212-751-3333).

PAGE 75: Mustard and yellow striped paper, Clarence House (see page 125); antique hooked rug, Laura Fischer Antique Quilts & Americana, 1050 Second Avenue, New York, N.Y. 10022 (Tel. 212-838-2596); painted table, Portico Kids, 1167 Madison Avenue, New York, N.Y. 10021 (Tel. 212-717-1963).

PAGE 88: Striped wallpaper, Hines & Co. (see page 125).

PAGE 91: Wallpaper ("Hyannis Port Stripe"), Hines & Co. (see page 125); oil lamp, c.i.t.e. (see page 125); roads and railway map of England, Lyme Regis, Ltd. (see page 125).

PAGE 122: Alphabet blocks, Susan Parrish (see page 125).

NEEDLEWORK SUPPLIES

CANVAS:

The number 12 and number 18 mono Zweigart's Wichelt Deluxe Mono Canvas used for projects in *A Show of Hands* is available from many local needlepoint shops. Send all inquiries to:
Zweigart Fabrics and Canvas
Weston Canal Plaza
2 Riverview Drive
Somerset, N.J. 08873-1139
Tel. 908-271-1949

NEEDLEPOINT YARNS:

Paternayan 3-strand needlepoint yarn is available from many local needlepoint shops. For information on suppliers in your area, you may contact the following distributors:

UNITED STATES

JCA, Inc.
35 Scales Lane
Townsend, MA 01469-1094

GREAT BRITAIN

The Craft Collection Ltd.
Terry Mills, Westfield Road
Horbury, Wakefield
West Yorkshire WF4 6HD
England

NEW ZEALAND

The Stitching Company Ltd.
P. O. Box 74-269
Market Road
Auckland 5
New Zealand

CANADA

Kelsea Sales & Importing Ltd.
585 Middlefield, Unit 31
Scarborough, Ontario
Canada M1V4Y5

SERVICES

The following needlework shops supply yarns, canvas, and a variety of finishing services on a friendly and reliable phone/mail-order basis:

IOWA

Judie Phipps (finishing services only)
Quality Service Co.
3496 30060th Street
Waukee, IA 50263
Tel. 515-987-5264

MASSACHUSETTS

Helen and Dean Chongris
Stitches of the Past
68 Park Street
Andover, MA 01810
Tel. 508-475-3968

NEW YORK

Joan's Needlecraft Studio
240 East 29th Street
New York, N.Y. 10016
Tel. 212-532-7129

Erica Wilson Needleworks
717 Madison Avenue
New York, N.Y. 10021
Tel. 212-832-7290

SPECIALISTS IN ANTIQUES AND AMERICAN FOLK ARTS

The following shops and dealers in New York City have an appealing selection of American folk art and other intriguing antiques, many of which appear in the photographs in this book:

Susan Parrish
390 Bleecker Street
New York, N.Y. 10014
Tel. 212-645-5020

Lyme Regis, Ltd.
Elaine Friedman, Prop.
68 Thompson Street
New York, N.Y. 10012
Tel. 212-334-2110

Donald Hillman
Hillman Gallery
1 West 67th Street
New York, N.Y. 10023
(by appointment)
Tel. 212-580-1939 or 212-874-0220

NEEDLEPOINT CHARTS

From time to time, I do limited charted design offerings. If you would like to be on the mailing list to receive information on these offerings, please send your name and address to:

Janet McCaffery
P.O. Box 116
61 East 8th Street
New York, N.Y. 10003

Cherries

J. P.

A C

M. H.